MY BACKYARD

A Living World of Nature

MY BACKYARD

A Living World of Nature

by DOUGLAS WAITLEY

ILLUSTRATED BY JOAN BERG VICTOR

DAVID WHITE   NEW YORK

To Jeff
May he always keep
his boyhood wonder of nature

Library of Congress Catalog Card Number: 69–10443

David White, Inc.
publishers
60 East 55th Street
New York, New York 10022

Printed in the United States of America

CONTENTS

INTRODUCTION

*C*ome with me into my backyard. The area is small, just 70 feet by 30 feet, but within the border of shrubbery, trees, and flowers, there is a living world of nature.

I know that you will respond to the glowing colors and magic fragrance of the flowers and to the beauty of the tiny pond surrounded by its trees and shrubs. If you are sensitive and observant, you will be filled with wonder, too, by the story this patch of ground, this small body of water, can yield—a story that goes back to the very beginnings of our present world.

As you look over my shoulder, or through my microscope, you will find that each season brings dramatic changes—not only to the vegetation in my garden—but to all the living creatures that inhabit the area. And the changes reflect nature's intricate system so efficiently, so beautifully, that each blade of grass, each tiny insect, each animal, each bird is born, grows, and dies, to meet the needs of other living matter—and all fit into nature's great design.

All living things, whether plant or animal, are links in a chain that must not be broken or disarranged. Ecologists warn that if nature's pattern is violated through mass destruction of insects or birds or animals, or through the pollution of air or stream, the system under which we live will collapse, and man himself will perish.

Life is possible on this earth only because plants give off oxygen

1

through the process of photosynthesis. Animals, including man, absorb this precious element and cannot live without it. Yet the cycle is not one-sided, for animals exude carbon dioxide which the plants must have in order to survive. And this oxygen/carbon dioxide cycle continues, over and over and over again, uniting us with the plants.

Let us look into my pond and examine the dull green growths of algae from which so much has sprung. Near the pond you will see mounds of moss from which the first stems, roots and leaves developed, making possible the diverse species of land plants now covering the earth.

You can reach far back into the evolution of animals, too, without stirring from my backyard. The ordinary earthworm is an ancient ancestor of ours. He has blood, several hearts to pump it, stomach, intestines, and a rudimentary brain. It was this creature who finally broke the bonds which bound animals to the ocean. Somewhere in the dim past a daring earthworm crawled out of the slime that had held all animals before him, and burrowed a long tunnel into the drier soil of pure land. And it was from this creature that the two segments of animal life, insects and man, emerged.

This garden holds more than links with our biological past. It reflects the great seasonal tides that sweep the earth. While the earth hurries on its eternal voyage around the sun, the angle at which sunlight strikes the land changes. With the approach of spring, warm winds build up in the south and gradually bring warm air to my backyard. Sap surges upward through the tree trunks. Crocus, tulips, and hyacinths break through the thawing ground to begin a new life.

As the season moves on and countless flowers blossom, perhaps your delight and appreciation will deepen when you discover how particular flowers are associated with human drama. King Solomon's garden abounded with iris. Cleopatra slept on a bed of soft rose petals. Peonies were the favorite flowers of the rulers of old China. Hollyhocks were unknown in the Western world until the Crusaders brought them back from the Holy Land. Zinnias, dahlias, and marigolds were sacred to the Aztecs and did not grow in European gardens until their seeds were brought across the Atlantic on Spanish galleons carrying looted treasure.

When the orderly movement of the earth turns summer into

autumn and chill northern winds invade the bright green world of my backyard, the chlorophyll in the plants decomposes, making it possible for the yellow chemicals (which have been in the leaves all along) to turn my trees to gold. Butterflies spin their cocoons in the bushes. Bees and ants retreat into their well-built citadels.

But I am not worried about the approaching cold and bleakness, for I know that my backyard is well-prepared to stand the winter's siege. All summer long I had observed careful preparations for the cold months ahead. Imitating the plants under the soil, I, too, will patiently wait for new stirrings, for "If Winter comes, can Spring be far behind?"

CHAPTER ONE   WINTER

A winter garden furnishes the observer with many a paradox. The trees, stripped of leaves, look anemic and frail; the grass first turns brown, then is buried in a grave of snow; the flowers wither back to the ground, where they lie frozen. Everything seems to have come to an end. And yet, at this very time, life has never been stronger.

The perennial flowers are filled with the sugars they have accumulated for the push upward in the spring; the great taproots of the trees are crammed with sap which will surge through the limbs to burst open the buds. Even the animals are at their finest: the chubby rabbit who dozes in the lee of a snowbank, the agile squirrels who bound from limb to limb, the field mice who scurry beneath the snow in secret tunnels—all are heavy with the layers of fat they will convert to energy as the winter progresses. And so, far from being a time of death, winter is actually a period of great power.

To cite another paradox: land under a frigid blanket of snow appears bleak and forbidding—yet snow is one of winter's warming agents. Observe what happens when an unseasonal body of southern air arrives in mid-January, and the snow disappears. It is delightful at first. The temperature rises to 50 degrees, perhaps even to 60. Life surges back in this false spring. Blossoms burst forth on the yellow forsythia; slender fingers of the crocus rise up to grasp at the warm air; and the hyacinth nudges the moist earth aside to thrust its head—covered with flower buds—upward to the beckoning sunshine. Even the fat old rabbit begins bounding around the garden, sniffing at the white caps of the emerging tulips.

But then the south wind, tiring of its brief escapade, scampers back to Florida—leaving the buds half open, fragile leaves exposed,

and a garden in as bad shape as a livingroom after a party. The north wind returns, tearing through the fraying yellow forsythia flowers, blasting the unprepared crocus leaves, buffeting the hyacinth buds until they turn brown at the edges. Without the snow blanket, the wind can prowl close to the bare earth, nipping the sprouts that had believed winter was over.

Now the eyes of gardeners watch for the fan-shaped filigree of high flying cirrus clouds—graceful silver messengers announcing the arrival of the snow storm. As the sky turns dark, and then the snowflakes fall, we watch the accumulating snow with elation, for we know that it is forming a protective layer over our plants.

The insulating effect of snow is truly surprising. When I placed a thermometer next to a tulip shoot buried under a foot of snow, I found that, while the temperature of the air above was an even zero, it was 30 degrees warmer around the tulip; and scientists have found many instances when the snow was as much as 44 degrees warmer than the air.

The amazing insulating quality of snow is mainly a result of its loose texture. If a drift of snow were magnified, it would resemble a pile of jacks with air trapped between the spiked arms of each flake serving as a sort of dam to keep summer's leftover ground heat from rising. A common snow drift is about 70 percent air, and a drift measured in Finland was so insubstantial that a bank 25 feet high melted down to a mere quarter-inch of actual water! In a way, then, snow is an illusion, since the rounded drifts that seem to smother the winter landscape are in reality mainly piles of captured air.

The formation of snow illustrates nature's paradoxical methods. for snow is one of the purest and cleanest of winter's tools, and yet it is born of dirt—at least of microscopic particles of dust which are always in the air. Without the dust mote to cling to, the frosty water vapor of a cloud would remain suspended in the air forever. But when the first ice forms around the dust, a chain reaction begins. Other bits of ice adhere to the original crystal, and, as the minute flake grows, a six-sided, amazingly symmetrical pattern emerges. This hexagon reflects one of the basic principles of nature, for its shape is determined by the structure of the very atoms which make up each water molecule.

The next time a snowflake falls on your coat lapel, muse on the wonder of nature, for if you could trace the inward course of the beautifully sculptured spikes, you would find them resting on six quivering atoms—four hydrogen and two oxygen—that make up the paired water molecules at the snowflake's heart. One is never closer to the atomic building blocks which make up our material world than when he is gazing at a snowflake.

Man could take a lesson from nature's careful creation of each

snowflake. A great deal of time and trouble is spent in fashioning the artistic gem which graces our winter and protects our plants. The embryonic snow granule is formed in the cradle-winds that rock through the upper atmosphere. Nature then dips the microscopic flake down into the swirling vapor-cauldron of a stratus cloud, where water begins to adhere to the stubby spokes of the miniature flake. Then an updraft jets the flake into the higher, colder air again, where it dances on the wind as the newly acquired water solidifies into ice. This process is repeated many times, up and down, while the crystals grow in size and complexity. Finally, its weight enables it to penetrate the turbulent stratus cloud and pirouette earthward.

Sometimes as I sit at my study window watching the snowflakes cascade through the sparkling air, I try to picture what it would be like if it snowed only once in a lifetime. I imagine living through winter after winter watching the clouds scurry by, hoping one of them would burst forth with that rare substance. Then one day the first flakes would begin to fall. Stores would close, schools would stop their classes, and old and young would run into the streets to gaze with wonder at the intricately fashioned snowflakes. We would catch them in our hands and examine the fantastic shapes, the endless variety, the pure white color, only to see them melt into commonplace water.

Let us return now to my backyard—which is covered with a thick, protective canopy of snow—for this marks the beginning of the year.

CHAPTER TWO   SPRING

*T*he seasons are like great tides which ebb and flow over the earth. Slowly, almost imperceptibly, the tide reverses itself, and spring is born out of the desolation of winter.

The season moves northward fifteen miles a day, seeping through the chilly landscape in the thawing rains of late February. Soon along the riverbanks the snouts of the skunk cabbage shove aside the frozen lid of earth and sap begins to percolate up through the trunk of the red maple. The long shadows of winter dwindle, as if the sun, which climbs higher and higher, is burning off their tips. Suddenly patches of snow ooze away and in their place, like green velvet gloves, small luxuriant growths of moss appear. About this time we usually see through our still-frosted windows, frail little snowdrop flowers waving in brief triumph before they are decapitated by the English sparrows enjoying their first fresh food in three months.

The rebirth of life is truly a miracle, for the shoots which burst through the frozen earth are using energy captured from the sunlight which struck their now-discarded leaves as much as nine months earlier. This imprisoned sunlight, stored as sugars and starches in the root fibers, is converted back into solar energy when the plant senses the end of winter by the change in the temperature of the earth around it. In a way each plant is a miniature sun, heating as it grows with an intensity which enables many spring shoots to melt the snow over them.

Like a symphony which starts quietly, then builds to a crescendo, spring gathers momentum as February melts into March. Soon the spikes of the first tulips dot the garden. Then come the emerald lances of the daffodils, the sheaths of the crocus, and the bright red, tightly furled banners of the peonies. By mid-March the first hyacinths—spring's floral aristocrats—pop through the muddy earth.

Spring

These early weeks of spring are among the most important of the entire year. As you stand amid the sprouts—each hooded with a tough bud-cap like an ancient priest—try to imagine the precarious existence of our primitive ancestors.

In those days man teetered on the brink of a fearful precipice. From the moment he left the hunting stage, to live off cultivated crops, he realized his complete dependence on those mysterious forces which he hoped would transform the tiny seed-pellets (which seemed as lifeless as grains of sand) into wheat sprouts. In the fall he had stood amid the decay of the dying year and solemnly stored the seeds in a cool, dry place. Then came the bitter cold of winter and while he huddled in front of his log fire (aware that without the warmth of the timber, which had once been part of nature's living forest, he would die) he wondered how the seeds could ever survive. He wondered . . . and he prayed.

The world was a frightening place, populated by omnipotent capricious forces which controlled the destinies of man and which must be propitiated if they were to act in favor of rather than against the puny, defenseless farmer. The early Egyptians saw the seasons come and go with the mysterious rise and fall of the Nile. Egyptian autumn was not so much a change in the weather as a decrease in the water level, which left the ancient land blistered and dry. Then the grain shriveled, the fruit trees became bare, and the world seemed quite dead.

To explain what had happened, the Egyptians created an elaborate mythology. Back in the shadowy days before the pyramids, before even the wandering peoples of the First Dynasty settled in the valley of the Nile, a benevolent being had been created from a union of the earth-god, Seb, and the sky-goddess, Nut. This was Osiris, who married his sister, Isis, and reigned as king over the Egyptian tribes. Osiris reclaimed the tribes from savagery, taught them to worship the gods, and showed them how to cultivate wheat and barley. It was he who first gathered the fruits from the trees and trained the grape vines along poles. Yet, although the Egyptians were happy under the rule of Osiris and Isis, there were a few who were jealous of the god-king. The chief of these was his brother, Set. One day Set fashioned a handsome coffer in the exact dimensions of Osiris. Then, while everyone was drinking wine and the sweet beer that Osiris had taught them to brew from barley, Set announced he would give the splendid coffer to the person it fitted. After others had failed, Osiris, suspecting no treachery, lay down in the coffer.

Instantly Set and seventy-two of his co-conspirators jammed the lid down, fastened it with stout nails, and soldered it tight with molten lead. Before Isis and her followers could prevent them, they flung the coffer into the Nile, where it was instantly swept away by the turbulent current.

With her beloved husband gone, beautiful Isis sheared off most of her hair, changed her queenly raiment for mourning attire, and wandered disconsolately through the countryside seeking the body of Osiris. The earth, in response to her laments, grew barren. The spirit of death then descended upon fair Egypt, and even Ra, mighty sun god, sank lower in the sky until it seemed as if the daylight would melt away to be replaced by the horror of an eternal night. In terror the people decked their homes with rows of oil-lamps, which burned all night, in the hope they could thereby induce Ra to brighten the country as he had done before.

Meanwhile Isis continued her sad search. Far and wide she hunted, ending at last in distant Byblos (modern Lebanon). Here she found the body of Osiris, carried there by the currents of the Nile and the Mediterranean. Aided by Ra, Isis brought Osiris back from the dead. With this miraculous resurrection, life also returned to earth. The Nile, swelled by the tears of Isis, had already inundated the parched land, and soon the buds of the grape grew fat and the first blossoms of the fruit trees scented the breeze.

The most sacred ceremony in the entire Egyptian year took place at planting time, reenacting the drama of Osiris and Isis.

The Greeks, too, desired to insure that spring should return to replace the bleakness of winter. One of their most ancient and solemn religious rites concerned the Eleusinian Mysteries—torchlight processions, night-long vigils, communion with the spirits by drafts of consecrated barley-water—all to help bring back youthful Persephone, who had been abducted by Pluto, god of the underworld, and for whom her disconsolate mother, Demeter (Ceres to the Romans), caused the earth to become barren to share her grief.

But the plaintive legend of Demeter and Persephone did not

remain in Greek favor. The later Greeks adopted the more violent rituals of Dionysus from the wild tribes of Thrace; and the youthful god eventually became the most popular figure in the entire religious hierarchy. He was an odd mixture of good and evil, of hope and despair, of solemnity and unbridled abandon. He was the benevolent god of fruit trees, mainly apples and figs, and it was through his kindness that the sap flowed and the fruit ripened. The pine was sacred to him, for its evergreen boughs represented his will that life be eternal. The Corinthians made his image out of the heartwood of a pine: his face wine red, his body gilded, and in his hand a wand tipped with a pine-cone.

The resurrection of Dionysus in the spring became a time of great rejoicing. He became known as Bacchus, the god of the grape, and brought with him a riotous wine festival.

In Rome the Bacchanalian rites were so excessive that they were eventually forbidden. In Greece, however, the people gathered in open-air theatres to watch plays and hear the great poetry written especially for the reborn god. Thus spring became a period of deep and meaningful worship throughout Greece.

CHAPTER THREE

THE RIDDLE OF LIFE

The Cell

*A*s I stand in March amid the early buds of my garden, I cannot help thinking of some of the myths that were created by ancient civilizations to explain the mysterious rebirth of spring. Their identifications of life with Osiris, Persephone, and Dionysus are fascinating concepts, but can only be accepted by modern man as poetic symbols. So we continue to ask ourselves: what is life? And now scientists seem to be getting closer to the mystery.

With the recent discovery of deoxyribonucleic acid (DNA), they believe they have isolated the molecules at the heart of the cell. This twisted, ladder-shaped group of atoms is found only in living organisms and operates in exactly the same fashion whether it makes up the cellular nucleus of a simple bacterium, a tulip, an earthworm, or a human being. The current belief is that the first DNA molecules were formed in the sea as a result of rearrangements caused by powerful charges of lightning.

Yet once the possibility of life being created in some primordial ocean is admitted, an even more intriguing question raises itself: in what ocean, on what planet or in what galaxy? To those who think life is possible only on an oxygen-abundant planet like earth, scientists point out that plants such as bacteria not only thrive in a Jupiter-type of atmosphere consisting solely of ammonia, methane, and hydrogen gases, but actually grow in lush profusion! Donald Culross Peattie in his fascinating book, *Flowering Earth,* promotes the theory that the first earth life was a kind of bacteria which had traveled across space, living on interstellar dusts, until it was pulled down to earth by its gravitational force. To substantiate his theory he describes the work done by Charles Lipman who opened the heart of a newly fallen meteorite and found there organic chemicals similar to those of bacteria living on earth. More recently, scientists discovered that meteor samples brought back from the moon contained sporopollenin, a biochemical which forms the coating of spores and pollen grains. Thus it is possible that life may have started on the mysterious planet which once orbited between Mars and Jupiter but which, some 4½ billion years ago, shattered into the fragments we know as meteors.

But life—with all its implications—will continue to puzzle man for a long time to come. What strange urgings force the seeds to send out their root-fingers, the bulbs their flower stalks? Why does sap rise in the sugar maples each spring, when to do so in defiance of gravity's pull involves such immense labor? When you break it down, life is just an arrangement of carbon, hydrogen, oxygen, and nitrogen atoms. It is 80 percent plain water, and the rest is merely air, bits of rocks, and the stored energy of sunshine. Separately, none of these can be classified as living matter. Yet put together into the right order, with its destiny guided by that wonderful substance, DNA, and you may have a daffodil shining in the sun, a butterfly drifting with the breeze, a lark filling the world with melody.

Everyone knows nowadays that the cell is the building block upon which the body is constructed. But it brings one up with a start to learn for what a short time the existence of cells has been known. Egyptians, Greeks, Romans, Renaissance Europeans—all had to wait for the invention of the microscope. Yet the elements of the microscope had long been known, for simple magnifying glasses have been found in the ruins of Nineveh and Pompeii. But the minds of the ancients were not conditioned to probe into the mysteries that lay, quite literally, in the palms of their hands. It took the fervor of the post-Renaissance period to free the European from the fetters of superstition, the blind reliance on the limited investigations of the Greeks, and the rule of a religious dogma which allowed no questioning as to the way God's universe was laid out.

Paul de Kruif in *Microbe Hunters* has given us a vivid picture of the man who perfected the microscope. Antony van Leeuwenhoek, born in 1632, was a mulish sort of Dutchman, plodding, unimaginative, with little education. He earned his living by running a tiny dry-goods store in Delft, and supplemented his meager income by working as a part-time janitor at the city hall. But during his spare hours he indulged in an odd hobby. He knew that a magnifying glass made things look much larger, but curiosity gnawed at him: what if he took the lenses and increased their curvature so that he could see even smaller things! For twenty years this grubbing little man made lenses, small ones, some no larger than the head of a pin. He worked and worked until he had achieved results beyond his wildest dreams.

People laughed at Leeuwenhoek, but the janitor-shopkeeper did not care. "I have taken no notice of those who have said why take so much trouble and what good is it?" he wrote. And so he continued, becoming so engrossed with his odd hobby that he often neglected to eat. His nineteen-year-old daughter Maria, who took care of him, had a tender feeling for her eccentric father, and would allow none of the neighbors to scoff at him—at least not in her presence. But even she had trouble understanding his passion for lens-grinding.

With fanatical precision he continued to make lenses. Then, with equally great artistry he mounted them in oblongs of silver and gold. At last the great day came when he was prepared to look through one of them. We can well imagine his feelings as he gathered rainwater from a pot in his garden. Then, walking indoors, he placed the rainwater in a little glass pipe and put the pipe under a microscope. Wonder of wonders! In his own words, here is what the first human ever to look into the microscopic world saw:

> In the year 1675, I discover'd living creatures in Rain water, which had stood but a few days in a new earthen pot . . . When these animalcula or living Atoms did move, they put forth two little horns, continually moving themselves. The place between these two horns was flat, though the rest of the body was roundish, sharpening a little towards the end, where they had a tayl, near four times the length of the whole body . . . These little creatures, if they chanced to light upon the least filament or string, of which there are many in water . . . stood intangled therein, extending their body in a long round, and striving to dis-intangle their tayl; whereby it came to pass, that their whole body lept back towards the tayl, which then rolled together Serpent-like . . .

This was Leeuwenhoek's triumph! He had peered into a new universe where living things bred, fought, and died completely unknown to man. Among this living matter were minuscule creatures who had ravaged the human species with far greater effect than the fiercest conquerors. Compared to these killers, Alexander, Caesar, Ghenghis Khan, and Napoleon were players of harmless games. Leeuwenhoek alone had glimpsed the terrible environment that surrounds us, and is even within us, but of which we can know nothing without the microscope.

It comes as a shock when we realize just how short a span of time there is between us and Leeuwenhoek relative to man's total period of recorded history. The Egyptians began forming a government and planning pyramids about 3,000 B.C. If we let that date represent the dawn of history (6:00 A.M.) and if we let the present represent man's noon (about 6 hours later) then we find that the Greeks besieged Troy about 8:30; and Christ was born at 9:45. From 10:00 to 11:00 Europe was engulfed in the Dark and Middle Ages. The Renaissance began to stimulate European thinking at 11:15. It was about 11:30 that Leeuwenhoek discovered the microbe world—only thirty minutes ago using our time scale!

Within those thirty minutes, however, discoveries have come with unprecedented rapidity. In 1665 Robert Hooke first used the word "cells" for the smallest units of life. In 1727 Stephen Hales was able to measure the flow of sap, and the science of plant structure began. By 1774 Joseph Priestley discovered that essential gas, oxygen, and conducted experiments showing how important it was for plant growth. But it wasn't until 1839, just nine minutes ago, that scientists formulated the cell theory—setting forth the principle that all plants and animals are made up of cells and that these cells are the basic unit of life. At the same time the word "protoplasm" was coined to describe the living matter inside the cell. And it was barely five minutes ago that Charles Darwin published *The Origin of Species,* with its clear and thoroughly documented tracing of the evolutionary relationship of all species, that is—in the words of Isaac Asimov—"the most important book in the history of biology."

Now we take this knowledge for granted. Anyone may look through a microscope and see the individual cells of a leaf. We talk glibly about "oxygen," "energy," and "gas," not realizing that these words did not exist before the era of modern science. We make our gardens more beautiful with hybrid plants, yet the science of genetics began only a hundred years ago with the work of Gregor Mendel.

We are living in an exciting time. Scientists in every field are making startling discoveries. We understand our environment better than the ancient Greeks did—including Aristotle himself. And even the great naturalists John Burroughs and John James Audubon would find new and revealing ideas in today's elementary biology book.

Certainly no one in this modern, scientific world should go through life without having seen a cell. Especially when it is so easy. You don't even need a microscope. Just go into your garden in the spring and look closely where the weeds are coming up. If the weed seed is on the ground's surface, you will be able to discern fuzzy patches around the tip of the rootlet. These are root hairs—single cells. Although these specialized, short-lived cells are many times larger than those which make up the bodies of most plants and animals, there are some which are much larger. Those of a green algae, valonia, for example, stretch out for more than an inch; and a member of the nettle family is reported to have gargantuan cells—a full eight inches long!

Nature produces cells in fantastic numbers, particularly in the frenzy of spring when the fires of life must be rekindled. Harry J. Fuller, in *The Plant World*, estimates that a single apple leaf contains 50 million cells. To clothe one apple tree, nature must construct the staggering total of 300 million individual cells. If human beings could invent a machine which would make one cell a minute, it would take a battery of 100 machines a total of 5,500 years to do what an ordinary apple tree accomplishes in a single spring.

Yet man cannot duplicate a cell, for each is a masterpiece of exceedingly complicated structure containing a strong, well-constructed wall (usually six-sided), protoplasm (the fluid of life), and a non-living vacuole in the center which serves as a storage area for the sugars and other compounds needed to maintain the protoplasm. A typical plant cell would look something like the drawing on page 23.

But sketches give a misleading idea of a cell. It is not something static, quiet, passive. Far from it. The component parts of a cell are in constant motion, streaming like ocean tides within the pulsating walls. Donald Culross Peattie called the viewing of this streaming through a microscope something that cannot be compared to any experience

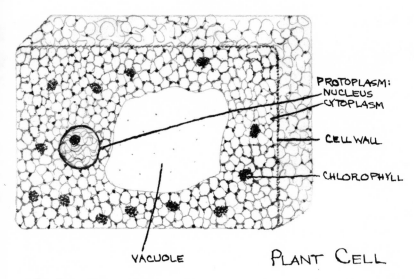

PROTOPLASM:
NUCLEUS
CYTOPLASM

CELL WALL

CHLOROPHYLL

VACUOLE

PLANT CELL

at the lens. The cytoplasm churns about, first one way, then another, as it reflects the mysterious rhythms of creation. The nucleus rides along with the current; the vacuoles throb in the interior, and often project narrow arms through tiny openings in the cell wall, thereby carrying precious food solutions manufactured by the chlorophyll to other cells.

The cell is a micro-universe all its own. The wall is composed of cellulose, nonliving matter that holds in the precious protoplasm yet at the same time permits food solutions to flow through it. In addition, the walls give the cell a rigidity which permits it to form tough stem tissue. The protoplasm is divided into two portions: the cytoplasm and the nucleus. It is the cytoplasm which carries the globes of chlorophyll that in turn tends to the essential work of manufacturing food. The nucleus, on the other hand, plays a more elusive role. Containing the immensely complicated DNA molecules, it guides the destiny of the cell—determining whether it shall remain part of the stem tissue, change into part of a leaf or into a segment of a flower petal.

Oddly, the composition of protoplasm resembles nothing so much as ordinary sea water—indeed, so great is the similarity that some scientists have referred to protoplasm as "the sea within us." It is intriguing to find in the protoplasm a link which reaches directly back to that era of titanic thunderstorms when life was created by lightning out of sea water.

23

CHAPTER FOUR

THE WORLD UNDER
OUR FEET

Soil and Roots

*O*ne must take nothing in his garden for granted. As the rains of April pelt the ground and turn it into material which gives way beneath the feet, you can feel the unpredictability of the soil. We call it "common, ordinary dirt," but it is neither common nor ordinary. In reality it is an extremely complex mixture of diverse substances, living and dead, which have been formed not only from the most ancient, pre-Cambrian volcanoes, but also out of the microscopic life which is being born and reborn even as we tread upon the spongy topsoil.

There was a time when there was no such thing as soil. Imagine the earth during those eons when it was cooling. The surface was liquid, composed of raging torrents of lava. Then, millions of years later, a thin crust developed, marred with cracks and fissures out of which rivers of molten rock gushed. Water could not exist on this frying-pan surface, and as soon as it fell it boiled upward in thick clouds of scalding steam which completely cloaked the earth's atmosphere.

A billion years passed—two billion—stretches of time so vast that the human mind is incapable of grasping them. Still there was no soil.

Finally, perhaps a billion years ago, the earth cooled sufficiently to allow the crust to jell into rocks—mostly granite. And the rain, which continued to fall, no longer hissed upward again as steam, but coursed over the rocks, tearing at them with insistent fingers, as it turned into roaring rivers rushing toward the gigantic chasms which would gradually fill to become the Atlantic and Pacific Oceans.

It is estimated that about 800 million years ago single-celled organisms began growing in the warm soup of the tidal pools—fragile, formless globs, possibly akin to the blue-green algae which still exist in the thermal waters of Yellowstone's geyser springs. And perhaps shortly thereafter, the first animals were created, living like parasites off the bodies of the plants—the only organisms that could manufacture food.

Yet while the seas began to spawn a teeming array of simple life, the land was sterile—and it was sterile largely because it had no soil. One day, however, a most amazing thing happened. Two completely different plants, blue-green algae and a certain type of fungi, formed a unique plant relationship which is called a lichen. Each plant benefited the other: the algae transformed sunlight, air, and water into food, and the fungi provided secure anchorage and storage of water. These odd plants were able to survive on the face of bare rocks—where even today they appear as grayish-green, disk-shaped growths.

It was surprising enough that the lichens could exist on the rocks. But even more surprising was the fact that the humble plant could actually dissolve the seemingly resistant granite! The penetrating acids which they emitted took thousands of years to flake away a single pound of stone, but gradually even the hardest granites were pockmarked with ever-deepening holes. Now rain water gathered in these holes, splitting the rocks as it froze and expanded.

As the rocks began to splinter, then dissolve into sand, the wind created vast dunes, which moved across the arid, lifeless countryside like things alive—slowly, ponderously, silver waves of a dry sea. Yet this still was not soil.

Finally the heaving oceans began to litter the sandy shores with the remains of their multitudinous life: rotting shellfish, immense mats of dead seaweed, countless billions of desiccated algae strands. Wind and rain mixed these organic substances with the sand. And thus the first soil was formed. But it was just along the fringes of the oceans— a thin ribbon of material more precious than gold.

Gradually, land plants began to utilize this soil. It was quite an evolutionary stride for the plants to adapt themselves to life on land. They had to produce strong roots to give them stability against the wind and to tap the underground sources of water. They must have sturdy stalks to lift their leaves into the sunlight and to withstand the savagery of the hurricanes. And the leaves had to have a tough outer coating to prevent the evaporation of the moisture that enabled them to carry on photosyntheses.

The creation of the soil indirectly played a part in the evolution of land animals, for the creatures of the sea could not leave their watery world until there were plants for them to consume. Therefore, it may not be amiss to state that man himself was created by the soil.

Once the plants began to grow on land, the process of soil production increased rapidly. Plant roots formed carbon dioxide which disintegrated many rocks. In addition, as the plants lived out their brief lives, then died, decomposed by fungus and bacteria, the rich nutrients of their structures became part of the forming soil. A cycle of new soil creation was begun which enabled the plants to spread until there was hardly a square foot on the face of the earth that did not support some form of plant life.

The importance of dead plants in the formation of rich soil cannot be overestimated. They become what is known as humus. This humus holds the rainwater; it keeps the clay from packing close together, permitting air to penetrate to the roots; and it fertilizes growing plants by releasing the organic substances of the dead plants. Good soil often contains as much as 40 percent humus.

When I am cultivating my garden, I pause to pick up a handful of dirt and it seems to me that I am holding history in my hand—for each inch of topsoil represents over five hundred years of growth and decay; a spadeful takes me back to the dawn of recorded history. There are molecules there that might have been part of flowers blooming before the Egyptians worshiped Osiris. A half-foot farther down and I am touching microscopic remains of vegetation that might have been flourishing when Cro-Magnon man began invading Europe, battling earlier Neanderthal man, while the north wind, fresh from the mountainous glaciers still covering much of the land, blew furiously about them.

I can trace some of the topsoil of my garden right back to the Glacial Age. The Midwest and the eastern United States, from a line that roughly parallels the Pennsylvania–New York border, the Ohio River, and the Missouri River, were covered by a series of four glaciers, the last of which disappeared not much more than ten thousand years ago—only yesterday, geologically speaking. These glaciers resulted from a gigantic accumulation of snow in northern Canada. As the snow reached mountain height, the bottom turned to ice; then, under the terrific pressure of the snow above, began flowing out like squeezed putty. As the wall of advancing ice plowed down upon the area now occupied by my garden, it scraped up all the loose rock it encountered, ground it up into tiny scraps, then redeposited this hodge-podge of gravel, sand, and clay in low, massive mounds which remained after the glacier melted.

My magnifying glass shows the rocky texture of this rich Illinois prairie soil quite clearly. There are stone granules of all colors: quartz glitters creamy white in the sun after I have broken open a clod of earth; iron compounds are dull reddish; shale is black; mica is speckled. Yet despite their different composition, the pebbles are all of a nearly uniform small size—reflecting the long centuries they spent being ground down as the glacier carried them southward from Canada.

After the glacier was gone and the weather grew temperate, the plants which gradually appeared on this inhospitable gravel withered and then mingled with the chips of stone. The decomposed plants eventually formed the rich humus that gives the soil its black appearance, but which I find under my microscope to dissolve into a fantastic mélange of minute bits of matter of all shapes and sizes. This humus, biologists inform us, is mainly cellulose: the remains of stems, leaves, and roots of once living plants. It is far richer in nutrients than the granular material, yet the pebbles are necessary if the soil is to have a porous texture which will allow water to seep through it rather than run off. In addition, the pebbles permit the upward flow of water through capillary action as well as the downward flow of carbon dioxide which the roots need for growth.

Most of the early cell production in plants is unseen, taking place in the soil. Since we see the world of nature from the ground up we have little conception of the incredible development that takes place just beneath our feet. John H. Storer, in *The Web of Life*, reports that the root system of ordinary rye grass grows an average of three miles each day—with an additional fifty miles of root hairs! And, whereas at the end of the season the grass he observed stood only twenty inches high, it was supported by 378 miles of roots and 6000 miles of root hairs!

Root hairs are certainly one of nature's most fantastic phenomena. The rye plant described above contained an estimated 14 billion root hairs, or seventy times the number of men, women, and children in the entire United States. It is these root hairs that absorb the minerals and liquids necessary for plant growth. The root itself is mainly a tube to carry materials upward or to store the downward flowing sugars produced by the leaves. The hairs are specialized growths erupting from the surface of the root just behind the root cap: that armored helmet which nudges its way through the humus and dirt granules.

I found it quite easy to obtain some root hairs for observation. I merely sprinkled a packet of radish seeds on the surface of well-dampened earth and within three days I had a dense growth of roots and the fuzzy hairs which cover them. If you do the same, look quite closely at the hairs, and you will be able to make out the individual hairs as thin, spider-web-like filaments.

But through a microscope the hairs become tubes, plump as narrow balloons, filled with water. Near the root tip, where they are just sprouting, they are small and straight. Farther back, however, they are quite long and dense, packed together like a thick, grassy jungle.

Yet even as you watch, the hairs dry out; they lose their plumpness and dwindle into shriveled hulls. For root hairs are ephemeral things, frailer than April snowflakes, drying in less than sixty seconds when exposed to the sun, and living even in the moist earth scarcely more than two days. In the hairs, as in so many other things in nature, we see how parts are sacrificed to the whole.

It is a different story with the roots themselves. Being permanent and essential parts of the plant, they have a complex structure. Since the only way to see the true wonder of a root is through a microscope, I have found a hundred-power lens virtually indispensable in my backyard adventures. Most people don't realize that such an instrument costs only $10.00 to $15.00. While my own microscope goes up to 430 magnification, nearly all the experiments described in this book were done under lenses of from fifty to a hundred power.

The root I examined was one from a sunflower seedling which I grew especially for the purpose because sunflower roots are relatively large. Using a sharp, single-edged razor, I carefully sliced the rootlet lengthwise upward from the tip for half an inch. Then I placed it under my microscope.

The view would have been quite surprising if I had not read earlier about the structure of roots. I could see the individual root cells laid out like corn kernels on a cob, becoming more compact as

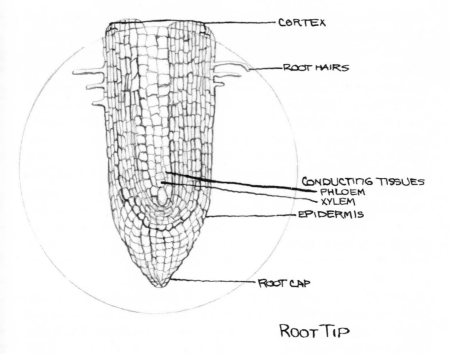

CORTEX

ROOT HAIRS

CONDUCTING TISSUES
PHLOEM
XYLEM
EPIDERMIS

ROOT CAP

ROOT TIP

they neared the tip, the area where they were manufactured. Along the center of the root cutting, I made out a pair of dark lines which started near the tip and continued up the root. They were opposite sides of the tissue jacket which would transport the water and minerals absorbed by the hairs up the stem to the leaves. In a sense here was the *great beginning*: the precise point where the plant commenced the operations which would result in life, if it were successful, or in death, if the root was unable to furnish the leaves with enough water so they could pursue photosynthesis.

Preoccupied with our lives above the surface, most of us do not appreciate the important role that roots play. Yet in many respects roots are the most durable portion of the plant, carrying it over the winter when the stem and leaves have died. Such plants as the larkspur, columbine, and hollyhock depend solely on their roots for future growth, and all of the deciduous trees—oaks, maples, willows—use their roots to store the food which keeps them alive over the winter.

There are two main types of roots. Most familiar are the long taproots that extend downward like tapered spikes, nailing the plant tightly in the ground. The taproots in trees are often far deeper than the tree is tall. Lois and Louis Darling, in *The Science of Life*, tell how ordinary, low-growing apple trees have taproots reaching thirty-five feet into the ground, and how a seedling oak only a foot in height had a taproot penetrating nearly five feet downward. Of course, this will not surprise gardeners who can readily compare the relatively small foliar growth of the dandelion to its massive root generally about four times the weight of the leaves.

The fibrous types of roots, on the other hand, while not so spectacular, have values of their own. The roots of the grasses, such as rye described earlier, form an intricate maze which does not go deep, but nevertheless penetrates into every nook of the topsoil. These roots, although weak individually, hold the earth in a viselike grip. The fibrous roots of the prairie grass earned the respect of the early settlers in Illinois when their iron-tipped wooden plows could do nothing with the matted roots. Settlement of much of the Prairie State had to wait for the invention of steel plows. Farther west, on the Great Plains, our pioneers, lacking wood in that wide, treeless grassland, found the fibrous turf so tough that they cut it up into blocks which they used as walls for their homes! Even today, grasses are utilized by man to bind the soil, for as soon as a roadcut is made through a hill, grass is planted to prevent the dirt from being gullied away.

War continues down in the soil between the taproots and the fibrous roots as they struggle with each other for the limited supply of water and minerals. The taproots would seem to have the advantage, for not only can they probe deeply into the substrata, drinking from watery sources far beyond the fibrous roots, but they can support woody stems and trunks, which in turn form extensive leafy canopies depriving the smaller, fibrous plants of sunlight. Yet even the mighty forest is not secure, for summer storms bring lightning, and sooner or later fire roars through the giant trees. Then, while the trees lie smouldering, the seeds of the grasses, blown by the wind or carried in the droppings of birds, begin to sprout. With amazing rapidity their fibrous roots intertwine in the soil, and quickly what was once the undisputed realm of oak and maple becomes a meadowland—and meadowland it will remain, for the taproots of the tree seedlings cannot penetrate the grassy matting.

Sometimes I think what a great experience it would be if I could shrink to microscopic size and descend into that weird, cavernous world found in the topsoil of my garden. I picture myself an inch below the surface. The earth would be surprisingly porous, with grains of sand appearing as huge boulders lying wedged against each other leaving large spaces between them which are only partially filled with the humus remains of dead plants. Roots would wind around and through the boulders and humus like giant snakes, and even as I watched, root hairs would grow out from the main root body as if they were thirsty little tongues. There would be large globules of water clinging to the boulders, many of them hanging like stalactites overhead. If it should rain while I was in my microscopic state, the torrent would cascade downward, ending in a muffled gurgle where it reached the water level somewhere below.

After the rain was over, a most interesting occurrence would take place. The water would return, not from above, but from below: moving slowly upward by that process called capillary action whereby water, confined in small spaces, moves up, drawn by its attraction for the surfaces of hard materials. (I have seen capillary action when I filled a long plastic tube with dry earth and, after placing the bottom in a cup of water, observed the blackening of the earth as the water moved up several feet.) Were it not for this essential quality of water, downward draining rain would leave the earth's surface desert-dry within hours after even the heaviest shower.

But I would soon find there was more to my underground universe than rocks, humus, roots, and water. There would be tubes of fungus everywhere, clinging like gauze to the surface of the rocks and the roots. To move about I would have to push my way as if I were climbing through a tangled underbrush of cobwebs. Once I grew accustomed to my environment, I would be able to trace one of these strands to its termination point on some piece of vegetable or animal matter.

(To get a good idea of what these fungus strands look like, observe them with a magnifying glass growing on a piece of damp, stale bread. They are shimmering silver, like silken threads. Under a microscope you can see the tubes with minute droplets of digested organic matter within them.)

Fungi are the chief agents of decay, and they perform an essential

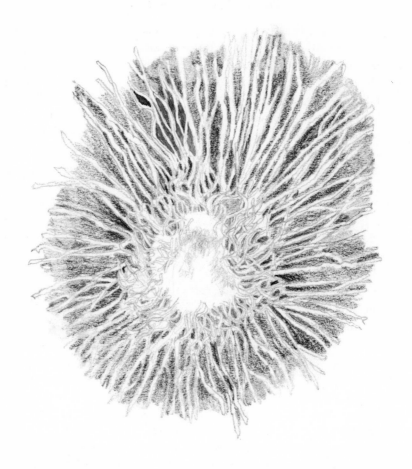

function in the organization of soil life, for without decay to release
the minerals of dead organisms, we would be living in a graveyard
littered with the leaves, twigs, and insect bodies of thousands of years;
and it would only be a matter of time before our mineral supply gave
out and life disappeared entirely.

Besides the myriad strands of fungi—scientists estimate that a
single ounce of forest soil may contain nearly two miles of their silken
tubes—there would be great colonies of bacteria, each a tiny (even in
my microscopic eyes) single-celled plant. They would be in a great
variety of forms: cylindrical, rod-shaped, oval, threadlike, and fila-
ment-shaped. They are the smallest living things—so minute that it
would take 900 placed end to end barely to cover the period at the

end of a sentence. Some would move by rhythmic motions of slender whiplike growths. Others would be found leading sedentary lives among the roots of certain plants. These bacteria exist in extremely populous colonies taking the nitrogen from the air, which circulates with surprising freedom through the soil, and transforming it into nitrogen compounds. These compounds form the small, button-shaped growths on the roots of the legume plants. These growths are called nodules and are conspicuous even to the naked eye. You can see them as light-colored warts on locust tree roots or as minute, roundish knobs on the roots of common yard clover. The nitrate nodules are another vital link in the web of life, since nitrogen is essential to growing plants, yet only the bacteria can convert the gas into compounds which other plants can absorb.

Aside from the quiet growth of the fungi and bacteria, there is a great deal of activity in the soil. As the roots grow, they give off carbon dioxide, and this gas flows upward, forming cross currents with air flowing down. In my wanderings I would probably come upon an ant tunnel—an active subway alive with ants carrying dismembered parts of carrion or plant food. And I would find vast numbers of other insects in the earth, for 95 percent of all insects spend at least a part of their lives underground as eggs, larvae, pupae, or adults. There would be grubs, which are actually beetle larvae, curled into their familiar disk shape; cicada pupae slumbering in a seven-year dream; the chrysalises of numerous butterflies scattered about like mummies. Everywhere there would be some form of life, for the soil, far from being dead, is full of animal and plant forms.

On my way back to the surface I might come upon one of the numerous earthworm tunnels. The worm would seem as large as a Chinese dragon, for it is one of the largest of the earth-dwellers. With its huge, gaping mouth, it would be gobbling up sand grains, fungus strands, bacteria colonies, and debris of decaying plant fibers like a vacuum cleaner. Yet it would move gracefully and rhythmically with pointed bristles securing the forward portion of the body to the tunnel while the rear segments moved; then bristles at the rear would spring up and the now-smooth frontal portion would slide forward. And as the monster slithered off, his tunnel would be partially filled with concentrated mounds, or castings, which form some of the richest soil known.

Emerging into the open air through the worm tunnel, I might find the world strangely disorganized compared with the compact, close-knit security beneath the soil. The plants swaying wildly in the currents of unobstructed winds, the birds fluttering this way and that in what would appear to be a lack of decision as to where to go, might seem too haphazard for comfort.

But that is imaginative nonsense, of course, for I am usually content with the life of an earthling.

CHAPTER FIVE

MIRACLE ON A WINDOWSILL

Sprouting Seeds

I am an inveterate windowsill gardener. Each winter—beginning in mid-February—I order my seeds from the half-dozen tantalizing catalogues that arrive in the mail. Before I open the first catalogue, I always vow to restrict my order to just a few packets—for my windowsill is not large. But once I see the pictures of the flowers in their summertime glory, I am lost.

There they all are: peppermint zinnias, powderpuff asters, basket-of-gold alyssum, double gloriosa with their profusion of butter-colored petals. I must have several of the endless varieties of multi-hued petunias. And there are the impatiens, nicotiana, and bushy balsam for my shady areas. By the time I am through, I have fifteen packets, a thousand or more seeds—enough to plant my yard and each of my neighbors' too.

Yet there is something exciting as well as irresistible about an accumulation of seeds. As I hold the packets in my hand, I know that I can create endless combinations of color and beauty. I have a sense of power.

I plant the seeds in small flats, water them with a fine mist, then place newspaper over them to retain the moisture. I fuss and fidget, but I have to admit that there is little I can do, for I am not so much a god as a mechanic who fills a car with gas and keeps the parts well oiled, but does not know enough about the inner machinery to do anything more to be sure the motor will run. I can only gaze at the quiet flats, impatient for the seeds to sprout, worrying that perhaps they are all dead.

But three days after the planting the first sprouts appear. Barely above the soil, they are real nevertheless: moss rose, sweet william, and celosia. Two days later the balsam and salvia are up; then come

38

the ageratum, candytuft, and snapdragons; and within two weeks all the flats are covered with the faint, green fuzz of growing things.

Now I don't mind if the winter winds howl outside, or if the snow piles up in drifts six feet high—for I have created springtime on my windowsill.

Here in the quiet of my study it all looks so simple: the seeds are planted and in a short time the sprouts appear. But a great deal of evolutionary trial and error had to occur before nature was able to produce the miracle of a single seed.

To understand the process we must go back to the dawn of life, when the very first green plants—the common pond algae—first appeared in the steaming, sterile seas. In this torrid world of bursting volcanoes and scalding, everlasting rains, the algae floated hither and yon in the ocean currents. Since they had neither roots nor stems, they were mere blobs, completely at the mercy of chance. The algae reproduction was just as primitive as the plants themselves—simply dividing into two plants. It was slow, but it was sure, and the algae gradually spread over the world.

It took millions upon millions of years for plants to develop into land organisms, for tough, upright stems and earth-clasping roots had to evolve first. But even when the first ferns unfolded their fronds in the free-flowing air, there were no seeds. The ferns, and all the lush forest forms that began to give the earth its first cloak of green, reproduced by means of spores—minute organisms of only a single cell. Because they had no food tissue, these spores were completely dependent on the wind to deposit them at the exact location where both sustenance and water were readily available.

The evolution of seed-bearing plants took place only some sixty million years ago—very recently when one realizes that algae had already existed for five hundred million years! But the evolution of seeds was a breakthrough in the plant world, for now reproduction was achieved with the greatest possible security through a complex embryonic root-stem attached to an ample source of food tissue surrounded by a tough outer coat which prevented mashing and drying. And it was through the amazing reproductive capabilities of the seeds that the flowering plants, which now adorn our landscape, were able to supplant the monotony of the green ferns and mosses.

But how exactly does a seed perform the miracle of transforming its stonelike heart into a vibrant plant?

It is a wonderful experience to watch the development of a sprouting seed. Take, for example, that of the sunflower, a seed large enough for experimentation. Split off the seed coat with your thumbnail and you will find a shiny granule, pale tan in color. A lengthwise cut through this granule will reveal the interior of life itself—the germ cells—from which all that blossoms on earth originates.

This interior pulp is not a uniform mass, as might at first appear, but it is divided into highly specialized sections. Look closely and you will see distinct divisions similar to those sketched below:

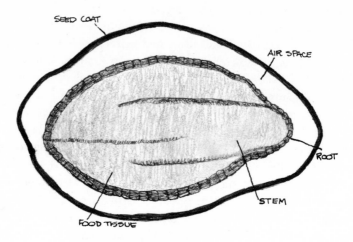

SEED IN CROSS-SECTION

This seed, representative of all seeds, is as complex as a rocket ready for launching. Everything that is essential is packed into the tough, little pellet: the fuel, or food tissue, which, just as in a rocket, occupies the main portion; the embryonic root, which is ready to probe, radarlike, into the environment; and the stem, the control center, that will take the energy furnished by the food tissue and use the leverage and water obtained from the root to propel the seed up through blackness into the sun.

To see how seeds grow, plant a dozen sunflower seeds a quarter inch beneath damp earth. A day later dig one up, and cut it open. It will appear like this:

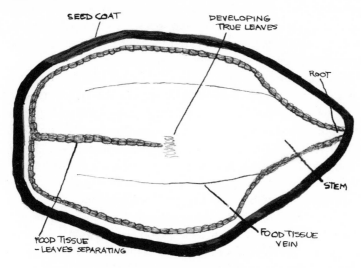

SEED IN CROSS-SECTION

The alteration in the seed is quite startling, for it has absorbed a tremendous amount of water—sometimes up to 200 percent of its weight! The water acts as a spark to set off the complicated mechanisms which activate the dormant seed. The food tissue has begun to swell and, whereas before there was an air space between it and the coat, now it pushes directly against the coat—which has itself absorbed much water and become rather soft. The increase in water means that the sugars in the food tissue can begin to flow toward the true growing area—the root and stem. Look closely and you will see the faint line of the twin veins through which the sugars are moving.

Another remarkable alteration has occurred around the stem area, which has not only swollen with absorbed water, but has begun to manufacture the folded growth that will soon become the first leaves. These leaves, seen as an indistinct, shaded area, demonstrate the rather surprising fact that even while the seed is encased in its dark shroud-coat, it is making provision for green leaves which will unfold in sunlight the seed has never known.

41

But the principal change has taken place in the embryonic root. With a sudden spurt of life it has grown to the inner edge of the seed coat, where it is exerting such pressure that it will soon stab through the softened shell. Run your finger over the newly formed roughness of the root tip and you will become aware of the mysterious *intelligence* of the seed which has prepared the root for its imminent plunge downward through the sharp granules of earth and sand.

When you dig up a seed the next day, you will discover that the root has exploded through the seed coat and the race with death is on. The root will dive downward, frantically seeking a permanent water supply. At the same time sugars from the limited supply in the food tissue pour into the root, enabling the manufacture of more and more root cells. There is drama here, for like an underwater swimmer with but a single breath between him and oblivion, the root must find sustenance before the short supply of sugar is gone.

All but a tiny proportion of sunflower seeds lose this race, for a quarter to a half inch is as far as the food tissue can send the rootlet lifeline; and once the questing root is deprived of sugar, the entire seed shrivels. But the knowledge of the terrible death toll among seeds need not disturb us; rather it should impress us with the tremendous vitality of nature who, in order to insure that just one seed will survive, sends a thousand rootlets probing downward, readies a thousand

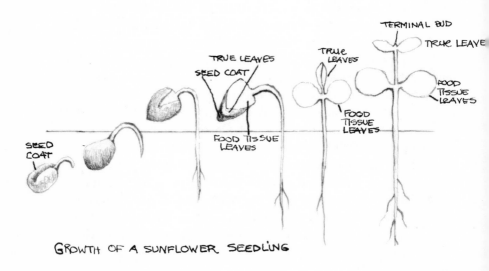

GROWTH OF A SUNFLOWER SEEDLING

stems to soar upward, prepares a thousand miniature leaves to unfurl their green banners in the sunshine. This is nature's irrepressible bounty, her amazing sustaining force whereby she provides that life, hardy and vigorous, shall survive and prosper on earth.

When the root has found water, the battle is almost won, for then this precious element can gush back to the stem, which now begins to grow upward until you will see it burst through the cover of earth. Free at last from the clammy darkness, the stem sprouts rapidly, although it is still so frail that one can almost see right through it. Soon the food tissue leaves shatter the seed coat, symbol of the embryonic past, and shortly thereafter the stem sends forth the first true leaves. At last the seed has been transformed into the growing plant and becomes one of nature's greatest miracles.

Although the roots will continue to grow, the main interest now centers on the leaves. As soon as the first glint of sunlight strikes them, they turn into factories whose sole occupation is the manufacture of food. Pick off a leaf and slice as thinly as possible across the grain; then if you place the specimen under a microscope, you will see something like this:

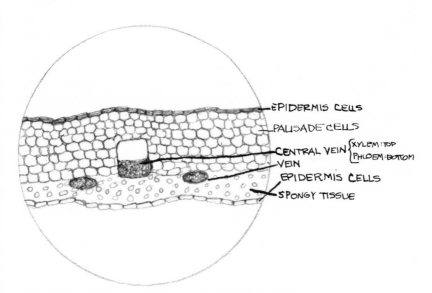

CROSS SECTION OF A SUNFLOWER LEAF

The tightly packed cells of the epidermis are clear, tough, and waxy. Their function is both to preserve the moisture within the leaf and to protect the more delicate cells within from injury. The epidermis is not a completely impervious coating, however, for there are hundreds of tiny openings, called stomata, through which the oxygen, carbon dioxide, and water needed by the interior cells pass. If you make an extremely shallow cut just beneath the surface of a leaf, a 100 power lens will show you these stomata as minute, straight lines, something like this:

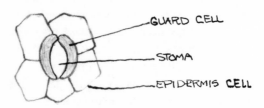

The stomata are encased in a pair of bean-shaped cells which contract to close the stomata when their water content is low. Thus on a hot dry day the plant pores are shut and the leaf is able to conserve its precious water most ingeniously.

Beneath the epidermis are the palisade cells, the most conspicuous part of the leaf. You will discover four layers of these long, finger-like cells in a young sunflower leaf—although most other leaves have less. The palisades are bright green, filled with emerald globes of chlorophyll, that quintessence of photosynthesis. It is here that most of the food-making takes place.

Next to the palisades are the mass of loosely sorted cells which make up the spongy tissue. Food is manufactured here, but another function of the spongy tissue is to provide air spaces for the diffusion of water vapor and gases from the palisades to the stomata, which are much more numerous on the under than on the upper portion of the leaf.

Scattered at regular intervals throughout the leaf, you will see the rounded veins which connect with the stem and conduct liquids to and from the leaf.

Most leaves have arrangements similar to those of the dicot sunflower with the palisades on top and the spongy tissue beneath. How-

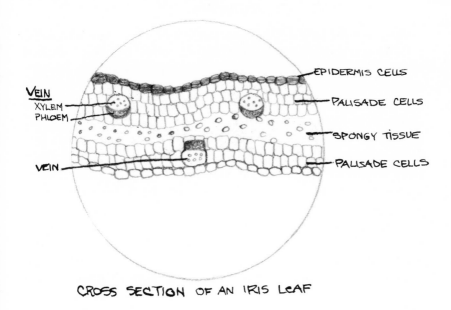

VEIN
XYLEM
PHLOEM

EPIDERMIS CELLS

PALISADE CELLS

SPONGY TISSUE

VEIN

PALISADE CELLS

CROSS SECTION OF AN IRIS LEAF

ever in the division of flowering plants known as monocots, where such leaves as those of the iris, gladiolas, and daylilies are upright spears rather than horizontal pads, the palisades are on both top and bottom, and the spongy tissue is in the middle. Here the veins alternate between the upper and lower portions of the leaf.

Although you and I may be the rulers of our backyard worlds, we can do little more than experiment with the results of that astonishing mystery, photosynthesis. Yet we need not despair, for even master biologists have never duplicated the food-making process from which all life on earth ultimately draws its sustenance. In its way, the tiniest leaf has an innate knowledge that the astute scientist with his electronic microscopes and battery of computers might envy.

The general principles of photosynthesis are known, of course. When sunlight strikes a chlorophyll molecule, it becomes energized and starts a complicated chain reaction which results in the alteration of carbon dioxide (which has filtered into the leaf through the stomata) and water (furnished by the roots) into a sugar called glucose and oxygen. The oxygen meanders through the spongy tissue and reenters the air through the stomata. The sugar, however, is either sent down the veins or is stored in the leaf itself as starch, which has the advantage of being insoluble in water and occupies less space than sugar.

There is an interesting experiment to prove that leaves exposed to sunlight actually manufacture starch. Cut a design into opposite sides of a folded piece of cardboard. Then fasten them over a leaf (I used a geranium) by means of paper clips so that both the top and bottom of the leaf are covered—spacing the design so light will flow through. After a day or two, pluck the leaf and remove the chlorophyll by first boiling the leaf, then letting it stay for several hours in common rubbing alcohol. As the chlorophyll is drawn out into the alcohol (causing the liquid to turn a beautiful green) the leaf fades to a pale, olive hue. Now dip the leaf in iodine. Iodine turns starch dark (as you can confirm by putting a few drops on a piece of white bread). If everything has gone as planned, you will see your little design outlined in dark starch on the leaf, while the rest of the leaf which had been covered and thus could not engage in photosynthesis, remains olive.

So we have confirmed that starch is produced. Do you also wonder, as I did, if oxygen is actually formed, as the textbooks state?

The proof is easy. I simply placed a wad of seaweed from my pond in a glass bowl brimming with water. Then I tied a plastic bag over the top, making certain it was compressed so there was no air in it. A day later the bag had begun to expand and within a week was nearly full. This was oxygen manufactured by the plant.

Or was it?

To be certain, I placed two grasshoppers in airtight glass jars. With one of them I put a sprig of seaweed in a small container of water; with the other, nothing. After several days, the grasshopper in the bowl without any plant life was dead. But the other, receiving life-giving oxygen from the seaweed, was alive and kicking.

There is something humbling about our dependence on plants. It diminishes my role of backyard monarch, for I am alive only because of what plants give me. As I strut about my domain, invisible streams of pure oxygen drift out through a billion stomata, seeping upward, curling like trails of smoke, losing themselves gradually amid the vast, oceanic tides of air. I am not any more independent than the lowly grasshopper: take away my supply of the gas that the plants supply so bountifully and I would succumb just as the grasshopper did.

Yet this dependence is not displeasing. Rather, it gives me a feeling of oneness with nature, since the oxygen that now courses through my veins came not so long ago from a water molecule by the action of the chlorophyll in some palisade cell. Even now I am probably breathing oxygen atoms manufactured by the sunflower seedlings with which I experiment. I feel that I am, in my own little way, helping to preserve man on earth by tending my garden. My backyard is part of nature's great cycle whereby the air we breathe is enriched so that we ourselves may live and breathe out the carbon dioxide the plants need to continue photosynthesis. I am part of that miracle we call life that encompasses all living things the world over. I receive comfort from that thought.

CHAPTER SIX

DANCING SKYSCRAPER

The Stem

*M*an has never created a skyscraper to match the seemingly frail seedlings I grow on my windowsill. Were he to use blocks of granite six feet square in place of the hollow cells nature prefers, his building would have to soar 180 stories to reach the same proportionate height as a twelve-inch stem. Such a building, again on the same scale as a stem, would be only 36 feet wide and would surely topple in any but the mildest wind. Yet these marvelous stems resist blustery gales and the most pelting spring rains.

The stem cells, under the guidance of the DNA molecules in the nucleus, diversify into many different types, each with specific functions. When the stem first breaks through the earth, the cells formed are small, thin-walled, nearly cubical. They divide with great rapidity, thereby enabling the stem to leap upward. And fluids flow easily through their soft walls.

Yet this very softness and quick-growing pliability would prove detrimental to the stem when it grew to a height where it could be buffeted by the wind and rain. Therefore other types of cells begin to form: thick-walled ones in the stem's interior to provide a tough, woody support for the rising stalk; elongated ones farther out which develop into tubes for the upward passage of water absorbed by the roots; rough ones that become the protective armor known as bark.

Since a microscope is essential in examining the inner mechanisms of stems, I again urge you to purchase a hundred power instrument. Then go into your yard and gather a handful of stems, as I did: sunflower, zinnia, petunia, pansy, gladiola, and a twig from a crab-apple tree. With a sharp razor blade make as thin a slice across the stem as possible. Place the specimen under your lens and be prepared for a surprise.

Far from being an uninteresting blob of uniform greenery as it appears to the naked eye, a stem is a mass of highly specialized cells grouped in arrangements so particular to each type of plant that a trained observer can tell what flower it came from with far greater ease than the FBI can identify human beings by their fingerprints.

The stem of the upper portion of a sunflower appears something like this:

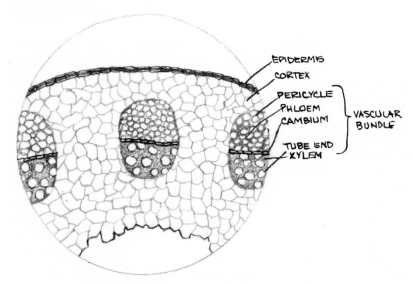

CROSS SECTION OF A SUNFLOWER STEM

The epidermis, or what is commonly called the skin of the stem, is composed of a single layer of small cells, actually colorless, but so tightly packed that they appear dark under the microscope. The cell walls are thick and contain a waxy, waterproof substance on their outer portions. The purpose of the tough epidermis is both to protect the softer interior cells from injury and to keep the precious moisture in the stem from evaporating.

Next to the epidermis are the cortex cells: large and pale green. They are related to the food-making palisade cells of the leaf, though in the stem they engage in a minimum of photosynthesis. Those cortex cells near the center die and become the chalky-colored pith which can be seen without a lens. Beyond the pith the stem is completely hollow. This hollowness, far from being a weakness, is a strength, for the large cortex cells provide enough support for the towering stem and to fill the center with more cells would be a waste of precious time and energy for an annual which must complete its entire seedling-to-seed-bearing cycle in the hurry-up growing time of a single summer. Indeed, the invention of the pith by the annual plants has caused botanists to place them a rung above the woody trees in the ladder of evolution—for the trees have not learned to avoid the needless creation of a cumbersome, wooden scaffold upon which to hang their leaves.

The most interesting portions of the stem are the vascular bundles, discerned without a microscope as minute, whitish dots on the outer portion of the stem—but appearing as large growths containing highly differentiated cells when under 50 to 100 magnification. A lens shows the outer part of the bundles to consist of very closely spaced cells, gray in color and resembling nothing so much as a mass of tiny bubbles. This is the pericycle, which, under proper conditions, sends shoots out through the stem walls to form the branch roots so obvious in ivy. The pericycle is also responsible for the rootlets which spring from stem cuttings of such flowers as roses, geraniums, coleus, chrysanthemums—and many varieties of these plants are propagated mainly by the pericycle roots.

Immediately behind the pericycle is the phloem: pale yellow cells with thin walls through which the food manufactured in the leaves moves downward to nourish the roots and maintain the vitality of cells throughout the plant. The phloem cells have minute perforations at their ends through which the sugars move, and are thus aptly named sieve tubes. Since the phloem and pericycle are almost always found together, I shall use the word "phloem" to refer to both of them in the diagrams which follow.

Next to the phloem you will see a thin, olive-green layer of cells. This is the cambium: the most important area in the entire stem, for from it all the other cells are created. Guided by the DNA composition of the nucleus, the cambium cells gradually alter to form part of the cortex, the phloem, or the xylem, as the case might be. It is here that the actual process of creation takes on its most mystifying aspect. When a certain type of cell is needed, the cambium will form that particular cell. Brainless, unthinking, without the slightest degree of intelligence, the cambium nevertheless is ready to fulfill the need when it arises—is actually working on the proper cell *before* the need arises.

Inward from the cambium are the tannish xylem cells. Whereas the sieve tubes of phloem are right for the slow, measured movement of the thick sugars produced by the leaves, the xylem must provide for the rapid up-flow of water absorbed by the roots and demanded by the leaves. In order to handle this much greater volume, certain of the xylem cells commit a kind of suicide so that the rest of the plant may live. These cells merge their walls, permit their ends to disintegrate, then die. What remains are long, narrow tubes up which the water courses. These tubes are easily seen through a microscope as circular holes in the midst of the xylem tissue. Occasionally you can even detect the bursting of a bubble of water that was in the tube when it was cut off from the rest of the stem.

An intriguing feature of the xylem tubes is that before each cell dies it makes provision for being converted into a tube by reinforcing its inner portions with a series of cellulose rings, which are spaced at regular intervals along the tube wall. A crosscut does not show these rings, but by slicing vertically down the stem you will eventually expose a long xylem tube. Through a 100 power lens you will see the rings quite clearly, spaced almost like bracelets on a lady's arm.

The stems of most other flowers are similar to those of the sunflower, though each has its own particular variation. In the zinnia, for example, the vascular bundles are closer together than with the sunflower, but they are not so regularly spaced. In addition, the xylem is fuzzy in outline and the tube ends indistinct. The phloem, however, is a pretty emerald green. A smaller portion of the center is hollow.

In the petunia the vascular bundles have merged into continuous bands around the stem interior. Here, it is the phloem that is hard to distinguish, whereas the xylem is obvious by its gray color. The pith is composed of large, rocky-appearing, colorless cells that fill the entire space.

Far different from the petunia stem, that of the pansy is more than 85 percent hollow—even near the flower tips where one would expect a more compact growth. The vascular bundles are regularly spaced, just as with the sunflower, but the phloem is difficult to make

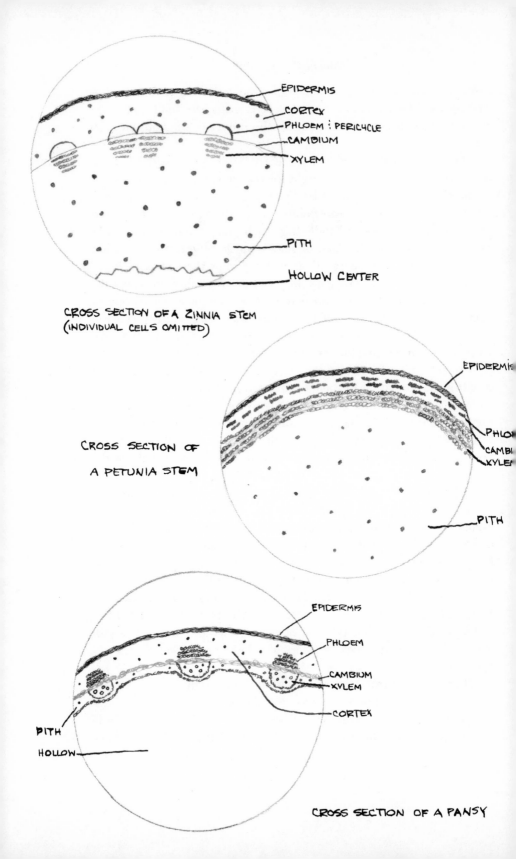

EPIDERMIS
CORTEX
PHLOEM : PERICYCLE
CAMBIUM
XYLEM

PITH

HOLLOW CENTER

CROSS SECTION OF A ZINNIA STEM
(INDIVIDUAL CELLS OMITTED)

EPIDERMIS

PHLO
CAMBI
XYLE

CROSS SECTION OF
A PETUNIA STEM

PITH

EPIDERMIS
PHLOEM

CAMBIUM
XYLEM

CORTEX

PITH

HOLLOW

CROSS SECTION OF A PANSY

out. However, the xylem is well defined, darkish in color, and the tube ends are clearly visible.

Whereas the stems of all the foregoing plants are annual affairs, a crosscut from the tip of a tree twig shows the startling difference found in a woody perennial plant. In late August my crab apple had accumulated nearly one growing season's wood, and showed the following features:

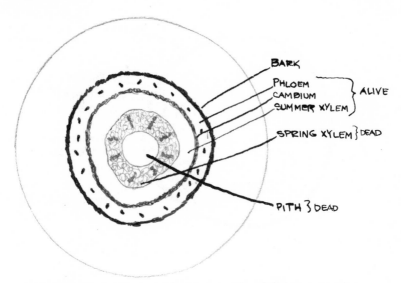

CROSS SECTION OF 6 MONTH CRAB APPLE TWIG

The makeup of the stem is essentially the same as for the annual flowers: there is a band of phloem to conduct the food material downward, a band of xylem for the upward passage of water, and the all-important cambium which manufactures phloem cells from its outer portion and xylem cells from its inner portion. However, because the destiny of a twig is not to die in the fall, but to grow year by year until it is many inches wide, both the phloem and xylem have additional functions besides the conduction of liquids.

The older phloem is pushed outward by the expansion of the twig, where it toughens into bark. The xylem cells, on the other hand, remain where they are to form the woody interior of the twig. During the spring, the xylem cells grow rapidly and the large-celled wood they make is darkish in color. With the coming of summer the growth rate diminishes rather abruptly and the summer wood is composed of smaller cells lighter in color. The following spring, growth resumes with large, dark cells. Thus there is a pattern of dark and light bands which gives the age of the tree. A crosscut from a segment of the same twig which is one year older shows these annual rings:

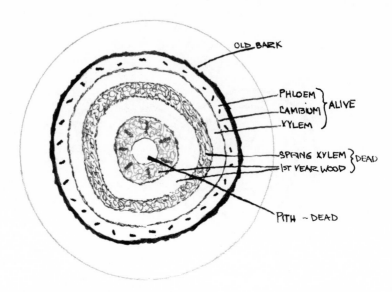

OLD BARK

PHLOEM
CAMBIUM } ALIVE
XYLEM

SPRING XYLEM } DEAD
1ST YEAR WOOD

PITH — DEAD

CROSS SECTION OF 1½ YEAR- OLD CRAB APPLE TREE

There are now two dark rings and the portion of the twig which is actually alive has moved outward. As year follows year and the woody, dead portion accumulates, only an increasingly narrow portion of the twig (which eventually becomes a limb) will be alive. This accounts for the fact that it is possible to kill a huge tree merely by slicing through the thin band of living material around the trunk. Midwestern pioneers used to girdle the trees which made dense forests on their homesteads rather than go through the laborious task of chopping them all down before they could plant their crops. The trees died, their leaves fell, and the land was open to sunlight. Then, winter after winter, the farmers could fell the dead timber at their leisure, using horses to slide the logs through the snow—a far easier method than pulling them over summer dirt.

In addition to the vascular bundle variations described above, I should point out that in case you happen to slice the stem of a monocot (such as a gladiola, iris, tulip, or daylily) you will find the bands of phloem-cambium-xylem replaced by circular growths distributed throughout the stem. This is because these plants are an entirely separate division of the flowers. Although more will be said later on of the monocots and how they differ from the dicots (such as the sunflower) let me say here that the arrangement they display is generally considered an improvement over the dicot rings.

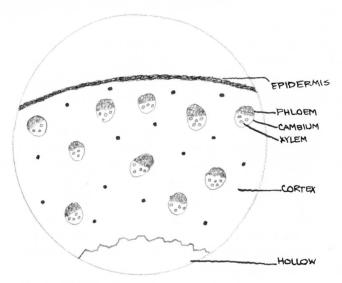

CROSS SECTION OF A GLADIOLA STEM

While each stem cell is an independent entity, all cooperate in the most amazing way. One of the most interesting facets of plant life is how the cells of the leaf are able to obtain water through the stem. This upward flow of liquid through the xylem tubes defies gravity, of course, and occurs as a result of what biologists call imbibition: the process by which living protoplasm within a cell soaks up liquids from impinging cells which are wetter than they (you can see a similar process when cotton fibers absorb water). Thus, as the leaves transpire water into the air, their cells, becoming dryer, take water from the damper xylem cells nearby. Each xylem cell or group of cells proceeds to absorb water from its neighbor until the most distant root hair, buried deep in the earth, has responded to the tug of the skyward leaves.

Because the leaves are frightfully wasteful of water, utilizing perhaps 10 percent of that which reaches them for photosynthesis, this upward flow of water is of startling proportions. To determine just how much water certain of my garden flowers used daily, I potted eleven plants. After I had saturated the roots and surrounding dirt with water, I put the pots in plastic bags and tied the bag tops around the base of the flower stems. Thus the leaves would be exposed to the open air, but the only water they could transpire would come from that already in the pots.

After twenty-four hours in a partially shaded location, I removed the plastic bags and put each pot into a container filled with an amount of water I had weighed on my postal scale. Then I compared the weight of the water absorbed with the weight of the plants (with the dirt removed). The results were astonishing.

A gladiola just past flowering used an amount of water equal to 14 percent of its weight. For a man of 150 pounds to consume that much he would have to drink 10½ quarts of liquid daily! A gladiola in flower used 19 percent, and so did a bushy ageratum in flower. A plug of grass was even more wasteful (37 percent), as was a petunia (50 percent), and a perennial aster (60 percent), and a mum (67 percent). Most surprising, however, were a blue salvia which transpired a full 75 percent of its weight in a single day, and a nicotiana which used up an even 100 percent.

I thought a marigold must surely hold the record when I discovered that it had transpired an amount of water double its weight, but then I measured a tiny sprig of ivy only to find that the plant had consumed over 400 percent of its weight in twenty-four hours! Just a little figuring indicated that if a man were to drink as much liquid as an ivy plant, he would have to down a large glass of water every minute of every waking hour. Water would be pouring from his skin, and his clothes would be soaking wet as his body tried to pass the huge amount of water into the air.

Yet it is not the plants' fault that they waste so much water. Rather it is the fault of imbibition. The capabilities of this liquid-absorbing process are far greater than the plants can use—yet it is the only method available. Edwin Way Teale, reporting an experiment which measured the stupendous force of imbibition, wrote that the pressure generated by the leaves of the humble tomato plant was sufficient to send a column of water shooting up to the cloud-dusting peak of a giant California sequoia!

There is a strange brotherhood among the cells of similar species. The vascular bundles of a chrysanthemum will furnish water and nutrients to eight varieties of mum flowers which have been grafted onto it—and each of the flowers will bloom. The cells of an apple tree will pass water on to the grafted branches of as many as 115 varieties of apples—and each apple variety will reach full fruition. A peach trunk will support a full crop of plums with no difficulty. And most surprising: the cells of a potato will nourish a tomato sprig, and the unusual plant will eventually grow plump tomatoes at its top while a fat potato tuber nestles at its foot.

It is strange how the cells of various plants grow in completely different ways—yet all presumably came from the same ancestor. For example, most stem cells grow in the prescribed manner: upright, one piled upon the other. They initially create thin-walled, rapid growing cells and later change to thick-walled, woody cells for increased support. But in such plants as morning glories and gourds, the stems do not alter their original thin-walled, freewheeling cellular construction. By using the trunks of other plants for support they

do not have to slow down to manufacture the thick-walled cells. This enables the vines to maintain an astounding rate of growth. I have measured several strands of a morning glory and found they each grew about an inch a day—a total of nearly a foot for the whole plant of a dozen strands.

But exceeding even the morning glory was a stand of gourds I planted one summer. When I left on a two-week vacation, they were about six feet in height and behaving very properly. But when I returned, I found they had indulged in an orgy of growth: they had climbed over my trellis, spanned a three foot gap, leaped onto my neighbor's roof, frolicked over his tiles, and were now peering down at him as he ate breakfast in the dining room on the far side of his house.

Other stem cells have developed in the opposite direction. Take those of the iris. The lumpy growths from which the leaves sprout (which most people call roots) are in reality specialized stems in which the cells have abandoned their ability for rapid growth. Yet even though they lie partially surrounded by earth, they still contain chlorophyll, and their food-making functions are essential for proper development of the plant. It is different, however, with the stem cells of the dahlia. These stems have carried the iris one step farther. Growing completely underground (where gardeners call them tubers and laymen roots), these cells have lost the ability to grow rapidly, or crouch contentedly in the dark earth, dividing slowly and methodi-upward, or to manufacture food by photosynthesis. Instead they cally, seeing the light of day only when we dig the tubers up to store them over the winter.

These, then, are the stem cells—those mysterious, dynamic builders—seemingly frail yet tough enough to resist the most vicious winds. In the spring the stem cells are produced in unbelievable numbers, giving credence to the various myths of rebirth.

When you watch the seedlings shoot skyward, you see nature at work, the most stupendous factory ever created.

CHAPTER SEVEN

GIANTS OF THE PAST

The Evolution of Non-Flowering Plants

*A*t blossom time my backyard is a mosaic of brilliant colors. The first of the seedlings I started in the winter have produced their flowers: white pillows of sweet alyssum, bright cones of candytuft, towers of crimson snapdragons. Perennial peonies form small forests of lush pastel blossoms, and interspersed among them are graceful nets of columbines catching the tufts of cottonwood that float by as gracefully as old New England clipper ships. One side of my yard is enclosed by a dense honeysuckle hedge, which in May is a solid wall of pink flowers with a delightful penetrating fragrance.

There are flowers everywhere; indeed, so overpowering is the display of beauty that one forgets there are other kinds of plants. Yet flowers make up only 60 percent of the 340 thousand species of living plants, and not long ago, geologically speaking, there were no flowers at all. Actually the flowers owe their existence to a host of other plants which began evolving in the soupy cauldron of the primordial ocean.

It is interesting how one can trace the evolutionary history of plants merely by analysing the growing things in his own garden. I began my backward journey at a pond I had dug near my patio. In May, before the pond sparkles with darting goldfish and bright water lilies, it harbors a fascinating, almost frightening, array of algae which proliferate until the pond grows murky with their massed bodies, and ultimately takes on an almost jellylike consistency. Bubbles of gas splatter up through the thickened surface and a slightly disagreeable odor begins to hover over the area. The pond becomes strange; timeless; a watery window through which I can peer back to the very beginnings of life on earth.

The first green plants must have lived in an environment like this: turgid, ill-drained backwaters where they could reproduce without being swept into the hostile depths of the ocean. And today certain of the algae still seek the comfort of such places. See the fine, silken strands, aquamarine in color. These are colonies of blue-green algae, among the very earliest forms of plant life. So ancient are they that Peattie believes they were created at a time when the sun itself emitted light in a different part of the spectrum, hence the blue-green coloration which is so different from any other type of green plant.

As evolution proceeded, some of these blue-greens banded together to form colonies; and these colonies produced a gelatin which surrounded them, perhaps to protect them from the changing light of the aging sun. I found these slimy balls of jelly, still common in modern ponds, appearing something like this when viewed through my microscope:

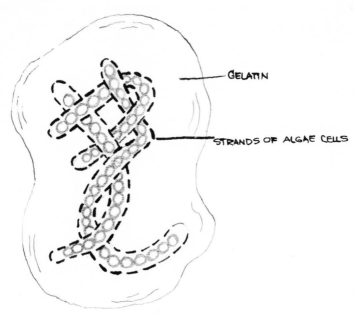

Under the microscope the cells of the blue-greens reveal their primitive nature, for they are simply a mass of protoplasm surrounded by a cell wall. The nucleus, so important in higher life forms, has not yet evolved as a separate entity—instead, minute granules of the nuclear material simply drift around the cell haphazardly.

But a pond reveals more than the pristine blue-green algae. A sample placed under a microscope shows all sorts of single-celled organisms. Some of these which I have observed many times under my microscope are called euglena. The euglenae propel themselves rapidly through the water by means of one or two whiplike append-ages, or flagella. They are oblong creatures consisting of protoplasm and lumpy globules of chlorophyll floating more or less at random within the cell wall. Although the euglenae carry on photosynthesis by means of the chlorophyll, which places them in the category of plants, they also have an eye-spot, which reacts to variations of light, flagellum appendages, which give them a surprisingly rapid method of loco-motion, and a gullet, through which they possibly ingest food. For these reasons many zoologists insist they are actually animals; and some go so far as to state that the euglenae, sketched below, are the elusive progenitors from which both plants and animals have evolved.

It is an unforgettable experience to watch the drama of the

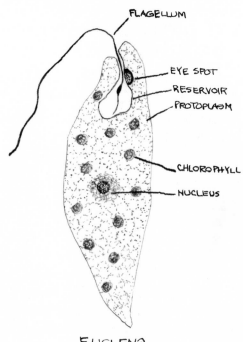

EUGLENa

euglenae as they fight for life in their perilous microscosm. I remember watching one of the little creatures as he spiraled through the liquid under my microscope. For a while he seemed to be enjoying himself, but slowly he became less and less active, as if he were tiring. His flagella fluttered ever more weakly and his movements were sluggish. I tried to figure out what was happening, then I realized that the water beneath the slide was drying up. But before I could add more, the euglena made one last convulsive movement—then exploded— the outer cell wall breaking and the globules of chlorophyll spilling out like marbles from a torn bag. There they remained, as separate and distinguishable as when they were held together by the cell wall, but no longer a living organism.

It is interesting to imagine what would happen if my pond were completely isolated from the rest of the world for 500 million years. One can picture the euglena and other types of algae coalescing into colonies in which the component cells gradually began to specialize: some developing into strong appendages, others into food digesters, and still others into a protective skin around the organism. Perhaps the evolving creatures would not divide into plant and animal forms, but, instead, would keep their ability to manufacture food by means of their chlorophyll while adopting the animals' superior mode of locomotion. Then, when millions of years had passed, a completely new kind of human might emerge from my pond: a green man who lived on sunlight and air, who did not have to kill to eat, who had the plants' passive method of living without violence or bloodshed. And who can say such a thing is impossible until the experiment has been tried? Of course 500 million years is a rather long time to wait. . . .

But the progress of evolution is so complex that no supposition, however well conceived, can ever approximate the bewildering wonders that nature has brought about. In my pond are green algae, higher than the blue-greens because their cells have a well developed nucleus. Who could ever have dreamed that they would discover the complicated sexual method of reproduction rather than reproduction by the simple splitting of cells? Yet that is the case, as a brief description of the reproductive life of a green scum called oedogonium will reveal.

The oedogonium is a delicate thread of algae easily seen on submerged rocks and on the stems of such plants as water lilies. Although the algae are undistinguished under normal conditions, when I placed a random sample beneath my microscope, I was amazed at their complex structure. They are composed of single cells strung together like beads. At somewhat infrequent intervals are cells of quite unique makeup. As shown by the diagram, certain cells develop male sperm. When ripe, the sperm break through the cell wall and swim freely until they are drawn by some irrepressible urge to a cell containing the female egg—sometimes within the same plant, sometimes within another plant. A sperm then fertilizes the egg by merging with it. Soon the fertilized egg moves out into the water. After a period of drifting, the egg divides into four zoospore cells, which scurry through the water by means of tiny hairs.

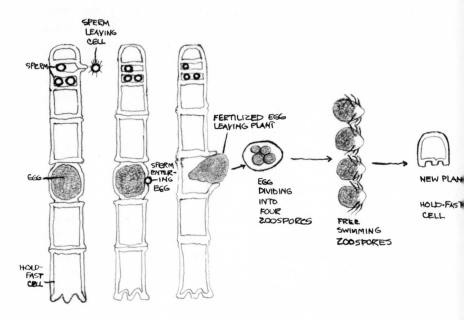

These zoospores are produced in such quantities that it was unusual for me not to see them speeding across my lens. At first I mistook them for unicellular animals, such as amoebae, for one ordinarily thinks of plants as occupying fixed locations. But, as with the euglena, we are close to the mingled beginnings of plant and animal life when we observe algae, so we should not be surprised when these early plants display animal characteristics.

When the zoospore finds a suitable location, it gradually changes into what is called a holdfast cell. It will stick to this favorable spot and soon will grow upward through the creation of additional cells.

The algae, primitive plants though they might be, are so adaptive to diverse conditions on earth, that one wonders what nature had to gain by creating more complicated plant forms. Algae can live in the scalding water of hot springs or on the frozen surface of snow. They grow on the bare, exposed face of mountains as part of lichen, or in the depths of the sunless ocean. They thrive as minute, single-celled organisms, or expand into gigantic colonies known as kelp over 200 feet long. They multiply on the moving backs of snails and turtles, on the stationary sides of trees and damp rocks, or exist in water with no support at all. In this watery environment, the algae ultimately form the food source of all aquatic life, and, with the exploding human population, they may someday serve as a major source of nourishment for humans as well. Studies are already under way exploring this possibility.

As evolution continued in those early ponds, certain types of algae gradually developed rootlike tissues which anchored them to the sand and muck along the edges of the water. Somehow the frail, filamentous bodies changed into stubby, rigid stems. Then tough scales began to protrude from their sides, forming the first leaf-like structures. With these rudimentary roots, stems, and leaves, the new plants were able to live outside the water—and to this day the mosses, next to the algae the lowest form of green life, have kept these successful structural innovations.

The lowly mosses: how you would have valued them had you lived 300 million years ago when they first began appearing on land. You would have sought mossy glens for relief from the monotonous, depressing world of rock, sand, and sterile plains. Compared to the lichens—those dull plants plastered on the mountain rocks—the mosses, with their soft, almost furry exterior, would be as welcome as a warm wind in winter.

Even today when I examine moss through a magnifying glass I am impressed. I see a charming landscape of long, velvety ridges clustered thickly with green spikes. Each spike is an individual moss plant, composed of many layers of exquisitely formed scales, green as emeralds, pointed as daggers. I can distinguish slightly different top-

67

pings to many of the spikes. Some are male growths—the more stubby ones—and others are female. And so, oddly, this jungle is divided into sexes, just as a crowd of humans might be!

The reproductive cycle of the mosses is one of the most unusual in either the plant or animal world. Nowhere is that phenomenon known as the alteration of generations more distinct. Reproduction occurs when a sperm cell from the male plant swims on a rainwater bridge across the tops of the spiked moss forest to an egg cell in a nearby female plant. Soon the fertilized egg sprouts into a new growth completely different from the green moss with which we are familiar.

This new plant, while remaining attached to the old one, is quite independent of it and consists of a long stalk, completely leafless, terminating in a large, podlike capsule which contains spores. As seen through a magnifying glass, the graceful capsules—green at first, orange when mature, maroon after the spores have left—remain one of a garden bedecked with Japanese lanterns.

When the spores drift off in the wind, they carry within them the ability to grow into plants identical, not to their parents, but to their grandparents: the fuzzy, spiked moss. A sketch of the life of a moss would show the unusual cycle like this:

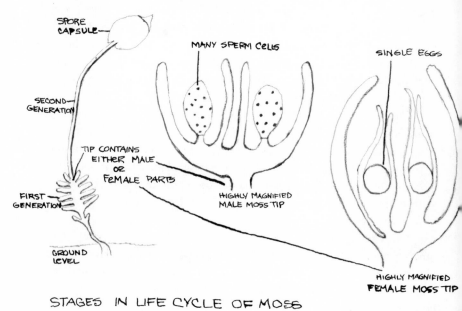

STAGES IN LIFE CYCLE OF MOSS

My yard is filled with many relics of evolution. One day I found four miniature plants, each less than an inch long, all but buried in the perpetual twilight beneath the weeping willow. Their thin stems were bent so that they lay parallel to the ground, as if they were afraid to attract notice. Their leaves, like tiny pine needles, were far better formed than those of the mosses, since they contained veins for the conducting of liquids. The resemblance to both the pines and the lowly mosses is so pronounced that the little plants bear twin names: ground pine and club moss. They are found only in shaded locations, and even there are rather scarce. Seldom do they grow more than ten inches in length, and it is believed that they will soon be extinct.

Yet there was a time when the club moss was a mighty giant, soaring to a height of more than thirteen stories and possessing a broad trunk six feet in diameter. During the carboniferous era the towering club mosses ruled the vast swamp forests, waving their lacy branches

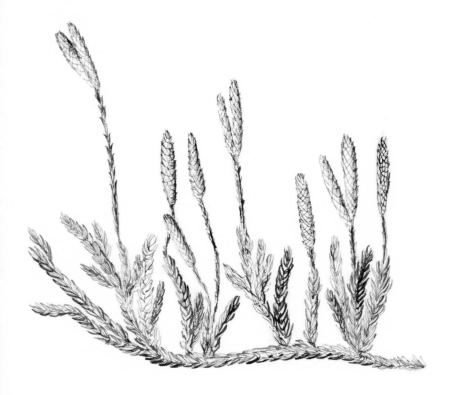

in the hot, steamy air. And when one of the giants died, the forest trembled with the crash of timber and the slap of water as the massive tree plummeted downward. Year after year, century after century, the forest leviathans plunged into the murky water. Countless tons accumulated, causing the earth itself to buckle under their tremendous weight. And now, the remains of these titans form the basis for much of our coal supply.

But their era has long since passed. To re-create their former splendor one has to lie prostrate on the ground and view them through a magnifying glass. They huddle close to the soil, humble representatives of faded glory, unable to venture out into the glare of the sunlit world they once dominated.

The end of my club mosses came with typical ignominy. When I cut back the branches of the willow, the sunshine was too much for them. One by one they died, until only a single plant was left. Tenderly, I dug the plant up and transplanted it deep in the shadows of my honeysuckle hedge. It continued to grow there for two years, eventually reaching the tremendous length of two full inches. But one afternoon a neighborhood boy, dashing through the bushes on some vital mission, stepped on the struggling plant. With its leaves crushed, it gave up the struggle. Thus did the descendant of the coal age monarchs perish beneath the tread of a five-year-old child.

Near the place where the club mosses lived their brief existence I now have a small cluster of ferns. They, too, are representatives of past splendor, although to see them huddling in the shade, barely rising knee-height, one would hardly guess it. Yet the ferns made a significant contribution to the development of plants by evolving broad leaves out of the narrow, pinlike spikes of the club moss. With these new types of leaves fanning out in a dense canopy, the ferns were able to capture a king's share of the precious sunlight. Gradually they rose higher and higher, crowding out the club moss, until they took over the coal age forests. In wild and lush profusion they grew, spreading wherever the nearly ubiquitous swamp lay flat, fertile, and inviting. And for millions of years the mighty ferns ruled supreme, for they represented the peak of evolution up to that time and none of the less developed plants could compete for sunshine with these broad-leafed, cloud-brushing titans.

But the dominant ferns had a weak link in their reproductive cycle which ultimately spelled their demise as the predominant plant form. Although their massive trunks towered upward like pillars supporting the sky, they were not able to overcome the odd alternation of generations which bound them to the mosses. While one generation caught the sunshine high above the earth and reproduced by means of spores (you can see these spore pockets on the backs of the leaves of the modern plants), the alternate generation lived as an almost microscopic growth barely a quarter inch in diameter pressed flat against the ground where it reproduced like the mosses—the sperm swimming to the eggs over a rainwater bridge.

As the climate became drier, the ferns, dependent on water to reproduce, gave way to a completely different form of plant, one which had been able to develop several amazing methods of dealing with the new environment. These were the conifers.

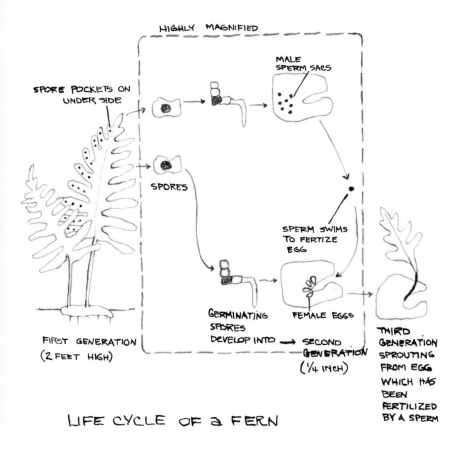

HIGHLY MAGNIFIED

MALE SPERM SACS

SPORE POCKETS ON UNDER SIDE

SPORES

SPERM SWIMS TO FERTIZE EGG

GERMINATING SPORES DEVELOP INTO

FEMALE EGGS

FIRST GENERATION (2 FEET HIGH)

SECOND GENERATION (¼ INCH)

THIRD GENERATION SPROUTING FROM EGG WHICH HAS BEEN FERTILIZED BY A SPERM

LIFE CYCLE OF a FERN

Few home gardeners realize the tremendous evolutionary advance which the conifers represent. Although extensive use is made of evergreens in landscaping—tapered blue spruces in front yards, sinuous pines along the sides of houses, columnar junipers next to doorways, and spreading yews beneath windows—people do not view these plants and consider their place in evolution. If they did they would appreciate them even more.

Look closely at a pine or spruce. You may be surprised, as I was, to find they have two different kinds of cones: some are large and conspicuous, quite tough, and remain on the tree often for several years. These are the female cones. Others are small and so soft that they disintegrated in my hand when I grasped them. These are the male cones. Each type illustrates the solution to problems which had hampered plants since the birth of life.

The male cone contains pollen granules—microscopically small singly, but sometimes forming such dusty-colored clouds in the spring (the word "pollen" means dust) that Henry Thoreau called it a "sulphur shower" and noted that the pollen covered Walden Pond and its rocky shores "so that you could have collected a barrelful."

Pollen is so different from the water-bound sperm cells of the ferns, mosses, and algae that it is impossible to reconstruct the complex chain of events that must have transpired as certain fern ancestors transformed the wiggling, semiliquid sperm into immobile, nearly dry pollen grains. And even once the transition was made, extra growths, or wings, had to be provided so that the pollen could be carried upward by the wind, drifting until it chanced to come in contact with the sticky exterior of a female cone. With the miraculous creation of pollen, the conifers broke forever the chain which had tied plants to a watery environment during the reproductive phase of their existence. Now there was a new freedom; and the emerging evergreens took full advantage of it to replace the ferns as the predominant plants.

The female cone represents just as revolutionary an advance. Peel back some of the cone scales and you will find a pair of seeds. There will be none if the cone is old and the scales have curled upward, ejecting the seeds as they did so. The seed, which results from a union of the male pollen with the female egg, is, with its predeveloped root-stem system, large supply of stored food, and strong outer protective coating, a great advance over the frail, single-celled spore that all the plants used for reproduction before the advent of the conifers.

Now rub your hand along the rough, ugly exterior of the cone. Here is a startling fact: it was from cones that flowers, the glory of the modern plant world, evolved. Does it seem impossible? Do the scales of the cone seem too hard, too immalleable, to be anything except what they are? Then go to other evergreens farther along the evolutionary line than the pines or spruces. Examine a bright red yew berry or a dull blue berry from a juniper. Soft as they are, they are modified cones. Look carefully and you can make out the scales protruding like frayed wrapping paper from the berry tips.

With the conifers we are on the threshold of the modern flowering age. Egyptians, Greeks, and Romans worshiped the evergreens as representing the force of eternal life—unconquerable, even when scowling winter descended on the land and the rest of the vegetation died. Our European ancestors also worshiped these majestic trees, and even today we recognize the symbolism of the conifers as we bring them into our homes at Christmas time.

CHAPTER EIGHT

THE RISE OF THE FLORAL EMPIRE

The Evolution of Flowers

*A*mid the perfume and glow of summer, it is difficult to realize that the many-hued flowers have the same function as the hairy caps of the mosses, the inconspicuous spore pockets of the ferns, and the rough cones of the evergreens. They are merely part of the plants' reproductive organs.

Most flowers are composed of four parts. As in the plum blossom sketched below, these are the sepals, the petals, the stamens, and the pistil. The sepals are the sturdy green cover which protects the inner flower as the bud develops. Although in most flowers the sepals serve no other purpose, in some, such as the anemone and clematis, they take on coloring, and open up with the rest of the flower to form what appear to be the petals.

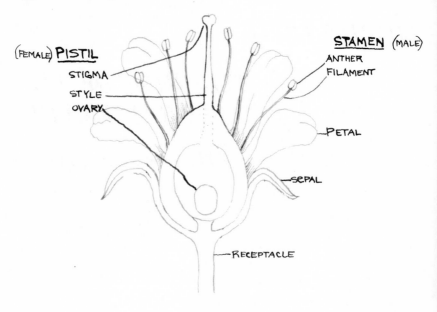

The petals themselves, like the scales of the conifers, are the least essential portion of the flower. Strip them away and the reproductive facility of the flower is not impaired. Yet nature permits no organ to survive unless it has a purpose, and the role of the showy petals is to lure insects toward the flower. In addition, many petals secrete nectar, the sweet liquid sought by bees. Others have been able to develop perfumes as a further lure to the insects. It is merely coincidence that most of these fragrances are appealing to humans, for some, such as the skunk-cabbages and a few hawthorns, imitate what seems to us the offensive odor of decaying flesh.

The male organ is the stamen. The stamens, containing cylindrical growths on their tips upon which pollen grains develop, usually hover around the upper portion of the flower where any visiting insect is certain to brush against them.

The pistil is the real core of the flower. The ovary at its base contains immature seeds—cut open any flower and you will see them there, tender, globular, ready to burst at your touch. When pollen is deposited on the sticky upper knob of the pistil, the grain sends a sprout down the long, interconnecting tube until it reaches the ovary, where it fertilizes one of the seeds. As the seeds mature, the outer portion of the ovary sometimes becomes very hard (as in nuts), or other times becomes quite fleshy (as in fruits).

All the flowers did not develop at the same time. During the dinosaur era, about 150 million years ago, while the conifers were successfully challenging the ferns, the first small flowering plants began to appear. They were haphazard affairs consisting merely of a mass of stamens and pistils intermingled with petals of various shapes. To an observer their method of reproduction would not seem to be any improvement over the conifers, for they depended upon vagrant, ungainly beetles (the more graceful bees and butterflies had not yet evolved) to blunder over their surfaces, carrying pollen picked up from similar plants. These early flowers were forced to have many stamens and pistils, because the voracious beetle often gnawed away most of the reproductive organs before rumbling off.

Yet the plants managed to muddle through, and many of these primitive flowers still grace our gardens just as they did the jungles where dinosaurs once fought. There is, for example, the peony, which reveals its primitive nature by its almost indiscriminate profusion of stamens and pistils. Look, too, at the columbines, buttercups, and anemones and observe how their interiors are crowded with golden-tipped stamens, and note that this very abundance places them back in the era when bumbling beetles were the only insects they could count on for pollination. Magnolias were probably the first flowering tree; and water lilies were the first flowers to invade the domain of the algae.

As the course of evolution continued, the early flowers were joined by others only slightly more advanced. These were the poppies, which reduced the proliferation of stamen to more reasonable pro-portions. Soon the poppies divided into other flowers found in the modern garden: bleeding heart, alyssum, and candytuft.

One of the most important and surprising flower groups appeared during those early days. Probably more than one dinosaur roared in anger and pain as he thrashed through a thorny bramble of wild roses. The thorns kept the monstrous lizards away, and the rose family not only thrived, but began to differentiate into many separate and dis-tinctive species. The small ruddy fruit that forms after the flowers are gone gradually altered into strawberries, blackberries, and currants. Other varieties of roses so greatly strengthened their stems that they became low-growing trees, while the small fruits became larger, more fleshy and succulent, evolving into apples, pears, peaches, plums, and cherries. You can see the derivation of these fruits by comparing the flowers with those of their rose ancestors.

Yet the amazing diversification of the roses did not stop here. Other roses began to produce strange alterations in their root systems which attracted nitrogen-fixing bacterial colonies. These roses eventu-ally developed into the legume line: beans, peas, and clover on the ground level, and higher up, the graceful locust trees and the sunset-lovely redbuds.

Shortly after the arrival of the multitudinous rose family, the early days of flower evolution came to an end. The earth went through a series of violent convulsions. In the eastern United States the land welled upward, producing the ancient Appalachians from what had earlier been eroded into a level plain, while in the west the youthful Rockies sent their spires cutting into the air. All over the world new mountains were formed: the lofty Alps in Europe, the Andes in South America, the massive Himalayas in Asia. The upthrust of the mountains brought a much colder climate, spelling the doom of the dinosaurs, and, at the same time enabling the flowering plants not only to re-place the remaining ferns and club mosses but even to compete with the high-riding conifers. Beginning about 70 million years ago maples and horse chestnuts started to rise above the pines, their broad leaves giving them a decided advantage over the needles of the conifers, while their method of reproducing by bee-pollinated flowers was more secure than the wind-blown method of the pines.

It was at this point that a new flower group developed. This was the phlox family. These flowers specialized to a far greater degree than those before them, for they molded their structure so that they would appeal to the just-evolving bees, more regular and careful visi-tors than the beetles. If you inspect any member of the phlox group —which includes morning-glories, forget-me-nots, petunias, salvia, coleus, and snapdragons—you will find that their petals are fused together and entrance to the interior can be gained only by certain insects who themselves have specialized for this purpose.

Probably one of the best examples is the snapdragon. Many times I have watched a fly or some nondescript bug try to nuzzle his way into the heart of a snap, only to find he was unable to push aside the firmly set jaws of the flower. But the burly bumblebee who followed did not have the same trouble. Like a woman shopper in a bargain basement, the bumblebee roughly shoved the obstacle aside and leaned so far into the snapdragon that she disappeared. Shortly after-ward she backed out, triumphant, her legs covered with large yellow balls of pollen grains. Through this method of selection the flower has assured itself of pollination, for the bumblebee always seeks it out, knowing instinctively that she will find fresh, unspoiled nectar within.

Open the jaws of a snapdragon and you will see how ingenious the plant is. As the bee enters, four long stamen are there to brush pollen against her furry body. Nearby is the pistil, its sticky knob ready to lift off some of the pollen the bee carries from other plants. There is none of the indiscriminate profusion of stamen found in the colum-bines, poppies, or roses. Everything is more purposeful in this higher order of flower.

Higher in the scale than even the phloxes are one of the most recent innovations of flowers: the composite family. Here the almost unbelievable has happened: individual flowers have banded together

79

to form a colony, all receiving nourishment from a common root-stem system, but having their own reproductive organs. Look closely at a daisy, zinnia, chrysanthemum, or dahlia. You will find that the head is composed not of one flower, but of many—each containing a pistil and stamens. The individual flowers around the edge of the receptacle (that flat growth at the end of the stem which supports them) have a long, narrow petal jutting out in a single direction like a sunbeam, and for this reason they are called ray flowers. It is these rays—each belonging to an individual flower—that we call the "petals" of the composite.

While the ray flowers are showy, the main job of reproduction is usually done by the more specialized growths, roundish in appearance, called disk flowers. In the daisy the disk flowers are quite easily seen, for they make up the entire yellow center of the blossom. (Notice how bright the disks are when the flower is young, but how they turn brownish as the pollen-bearing stamens wither after maturity.) In the zinnias the disk flowers don't occupy quite so large an area, but still form a distinctive, well-defined cluster in the center. However, the asters and marigolds are so luxuriant with ray flowers that few people notice the small collection of disk flowers seen only when the ray petals are fully opened.

The intermixture of ray and disk flowers, characteristic of most composites, does not carry through for all. A most successful composite is the dandelion. The sunshine-yellow blossom we ordinarily think of as a single flower is in reality dozens of separate ray flowers. Pull a dandelion apart and you will see that each "petal" is actually a ray flower enclosing within it stamens and a pistil. Eventually this ray will develop into the brown seed supported by the fine, white parachute which we see drifting in the wind.

Other composites are made up entirely of disk flowers. Although the disks are ordinarily the least conspicuous, in massed groupings they are sometimes quite impressive, as when they appear in the ageratum and liatris (blazing star). Here they nestle close together, the slightly protruding stamens giving the blossoms their appealing fuzzy effect.

Long ago the flowers divided into two competing groups. All of the plants just described belong to the division called dicotyledons, or more simply, dicots. That the dicots branched out from a common ancestor is revealed by the fact that they all begin life by breaking through the soil with a more or less identical pair of seed leaves, or cotyledons (hence their name). In addition, all dicot leaves are net-veined and their flower parts—most obvious in the petals—are usually in fours or fives.

Not so with the monocots. The young monocot stabs through the soil with a single, lanced leaf, such as the spear of the daffodil or the needle of the grasses. And the leaves of the monocots are quite different: long, narrow, and parallel-veined like those of the tulips, lilies, crocuses, and gladiolas. Monocot flowers are distinctive too. With their parts in units of three, they sometimes reach a beauty that none of the dicots can match.

Take for example that queen of flowers, the iris. Everything here is in harmonic triads. As the bud opens the three lower petals roll out: the outer portions a rich variation of a rainbow of colors (the flower is named after the Greek rainbow goddess), lighter on the edges, growing imperceptibly darker toward the center. These petals, known as the "falls" for their arching, cascading appearance, contain a soft, white growth toward their crest line which devotees call the "beard." The three upper petals unfurl into upright, translucent banners, known as "standards."

How wonderful it would be to walk down the perfumed iris chamber as a honey bee does. My tread would fall on a velvetlike surface, and the light around me would be a gauzy cathedral tint created by the upper petals which rose overhead like gothic arches. Moving along the tapestried "beard," I would pass the horizontal pistil column, hazy charcoal in color, leading down to the ovary chamber at the base of the flower. Color would be all around me: pale and diffused in some places, brilliant and lustrous in others. And hanging overhead would be the stamen chandeliers glittering with golden specks of pollen.

The monocots are fierce competitors, and it appears that the dicots are falling before them. In this battle, man is aiding the monocots, for much of our land in the temperate zone is devoted to such monocots as corn, wheat, oats, and rye; and in the tropics other monocots, such as sugar cane, rice, bananas, and date palms reign supreme. Although it is true that we protect the dicots, both by offering the smaller ones sanctuary within our little garden plots and the larger ones—the maples, oaks, and elms—refuge in our parks and on our city streets, nevertheless the monocots seem to be the coming rulers.

Perhaps within the next million years—after man has vanished into the stars—the ever-encroaching monocot grasses will have pushed the dicot flowers back into shady recesses where they will join the ferns and club mosses as living fossils. The dicot forests will last longer; they will fight back; and there will be many casualties among the grasses caught in their shadows. But autumns are dry and fires will start—and once the forest burns, the grasses will be there holding the soil in an embrace that no maple seedling can break.

The dicot day will end when the last tree, standing magnificent and lonely in the midst of the prairie, is shattered by a shaft of lightning and topples ponderously to its doom. Then, evolution will move on—perhaps to new, improved forms of plant life—forms so wonderful, so beauteous and bright, that we cannot even begin to imagine them.

CHAPTER NINE

BULB MADNESS

*A*mong Nature's most interesting innovations are the bulbs. Many of them, such as tulips and daffodils, are able to flower so much earlier than the seed plants, earlier even than the perennials that have had a year's head start, because, in a manner of speaking, they have been in flower all winter! How can this be? Because bulbs are really flowers encased by a thick growth of leaves, largely white and scaly as seen when you cut a bulb open. The diagram below shows the surprising internal structure of a narcissus bulb.

The bulb is composed of distinct parts. The outer covering is

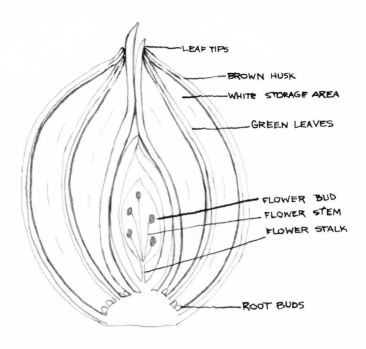

LEAF TIPS

BROWN HUSK

WHITE STORAGE AREA

GREEN LEAVES

FLOWER BUD
FLOWER STEM
FLOWER STALK

ROOT BUDS

made up of brown scales, tough and dry, which form a sort of armor to protect the rest of the organism. Next to this husk is a white, layered material which serves to store starches and water. Then come greenish growths: leaves already filled with chlorophyll ready to begin producing food as soon as they are exposed to sunlight. These leaves are attached at their base to a brownish root area, from which water and minerals will flow as soon as the roots, which can be seen as tiny, light-colored nubbins, begin to grow.

But the most important part of the bulb is in the center, where complete flowers slumber, like frozen flames, waiting for the proper conditions to send them shooting upward. These are not just rudimentary flowers either: they are fully developed, for you can pull them away from the sheath which encases them and they stand upright on narrow stems 3/4 inch long. The petals are so thin that they are almost transparent, but the reproductive organs of the flower are almost as large and well-formed as in the mature bloom! You cannot help but notice them: the pollen-bearing stamens, bright orange-yellow, and the pistil, with a slight bulge at the bottom. By slicing open the base of the pistil you can make out the windrows where the nearly microscopic seeds are already half-formed!

Each bulb has its own particular history. The daffodils, for example, were called the "king's spear" by the ancients, who were impressed by the long, narrow, lancelike leaves. The Greeks, when they dreamed of the glories of the Elysian Fields, that happy residence of their honored dead, saw a landscape brightened with masses of daffodils.

On the other hand, the narcissus has a more somber legend. One Greek story states that Zeus created the lovely flower to lure Persephone away from her companions. Since there never had been a blossom with so strong a scent the maiden could not resist running to see it. In an instant Pluto, brother of Zeus, was there in his chariot, drawn by coal-black chargers. Snatching up the unsuspecting girl, he lashed his steeds and descended into a dark chasm which closed instantly as he sped downward. And ever afterward the flower belonged to Persephone, unwilling queen of the underworld, and the Greek name for the plant, *narkissos*, reflects its unearthly perfume, so strong and penetrating—for the word means narcotic!

The narcissus family includes the daffodils and jonquils, so one

can never be quite certain to which flower the later Greek legend of
the tragic youth called Narcissus pertains. But the story goes that
Narcissus was a handsome young man, beloved by all the woodland
nymphs. But he had no time for any of them, not even for the fairest,
pensive Echo. Echo did everything she could to attract him, but she
had met with the disfavor of Hera, jealous wife of Zeus, who had
forbidden her to use her tongue except to repeat what had been said
to her. Yet she sought Narcissus and one day saw him in the woods.
"Is anyone here?" the young man called. And joyful Echo answered,
"Here! Here!" "Come," he called. "Come!" she answered, stepping
out to meet him, her arms outstretched. But Narcissus had no interest
in her. "I will die before I give you power over me," he cried as he
fled from her. All Echo could do was to mourn: "I give you power
over me." But Narcissus was gone and the heartsick nymph left the
woodland paradise to roam throughout the rocky places of the earth,
her body wasting away so that all that was left was her plaintive voice.

Narcissus could not go on spurning the nymphs forever. They
appealed to the terrible goddess Nemesis, the righteous avenger.
Determined that Narcissus should experience the sorrow of an impossible love, Nemesis made him enchanted with his own reflection as
he leaned over a pool to drink. And there he remained, gazing into
the water day after day, unable to leave the beauty of his own image,
not even for food. His body grew weak and he knew death was coming,
but still he could not bear to part from his reflection. At last he laid
his head against a mossy stone. "Farewell," he murmured, and Echo,
standing unseen nearby whispered, "Farewell." Then he died.

The next day his body had disappeared, and in its place was a
narcissus (or perhaps a jonquil or daffodil) bending its head over the
pool, still entranced with its watery image. And even today the plants
of the narcissus family love the shaded, moist woodlands close to a
trickling creek or quiet pond.

The crocus, too, appears in Greek legend, for when Hermes ac-
cidently killed the infant son of Europa, he turned the blood into the
low-growing flower. Because it represented the regeneration of a dead
being, the Greeks believed it had great medicinal powers—that just
to hold it would serve as a tonic to enliven depressed spirits. The
Greeks named it after the *kroke* or "thread," because of its three

threadlike stigmata. It was from these stigmata that the dye known as saffron was obtained—4,000 of the tiny stigmata being pressed together to form a single ounce of the dye. Because saffron was so costly, it was used only to color the robes of Grecian kings. The bulb (or, more properly, the corm) of the crocus used in the yellowish dye has a slightly bitter, though appealing flavor, which caused the Greeks and later the Britons (who became acquainted with the saffron crocus when Crusaders brought it back from the Near East) to use it as a flavoring for their food.

The hyacinth has a history equally interesting. Hyacinthus was a handsome youth, the companion of Apollo, the sun god. But Zephyr, the west wind, was jealous of them and one day, when Apollo was throwing the discus, Zephyr blew upon the flying object and caused it to strike Hyacinthus full in the forehead. The young man dropped to the ground, blood gushing from his wound. Apollo tried in vain to save him. The best he could do was to turn the blood-stained grass into the beautiful flower that we know as the hyacinth.

The Greeks had a special regard for the sweet-scented hyacinth and fashioned it into victory wreaths to be placed upon the heads of their heroes. The Romans had a still greater veneration for the flower, using it as part of the chaplets bedecking priests during religious cere-monies. Yet the hyacinth was unknown in Europe until the sixteenth century, when the bulbs were carried northward from the Mediter-ranean. Then they became quite popular—so popular, indeed, that it was a matter of some prestige to be able to afford a hyacinth garden. Among the Dutch one rare bulb even sold for nearly a thou-sand dollars.

But it wasn't the hyacinth which caused the greatest stir in flower history. This distinction falls to the tulip. Never before or since has a single flower species aroused such fervor in a continent as the tulip did in seventeenth century Europe.

The episode began in ancient Persia, where the flowers grew wild. They were formed, so the legend went, from the tears of a god who had stumbled across the desert pining for his lost love. The Persians took the common red flowers for granted, and even though Omar Khayyam mentioned them in his poems, little was done to domesticate and develop the tulip. Instead the Persians preferred to grow the more artistic rose or the ostentatious lily in the walled gardens they called "paradises," from which our modern word is derived.

But after the Turks conquered Persia, the land was opened to an influx of foreign merchants who were attracted by the many varieties of tulips—some counted thirty—which flowed like tapestry over the hills at springtime. Often the caravans would halt, camels snorting and shifting the weight of their burdens, while the master dug up some of the abundant bulbs and placed them in special satchels to carry back to the imperial capital—wondrous Constantinople.

The Turkish people, from the sultan down to the turbaned farmer, became enamored of the new plant. Never before had they seen anything like it—the brilliance of the colors, the dazzling effect of massed plantings, the grace of the willowy stem swaying in the Bosporus breezes. The Sultan's sprawling palace, the famous seraglio, became ablaze with tulips and the Grand Turk even went so far as to proclaim the tulip the royal flower and place it as an emblem on all official documents. Towns and villages all over Anatolia burst forth with masses of tulips every spring, and once a year a gay Festival of Tulips enveloped the warlike nation—an annual splurge of gaiety.

As the Turkish empire expanded, European ambassadors began arriving in Constantinople. In 1554 the Austrian Emperor sent a man by the name of Busbecq, who was astounded with the display of tulips which were in full bloom even though it was still winter. Knowing little of the Turkish language, Busbecq called the enchanting flowers "tulipam" for their resemblance to the ubiquitous "tulbands," or turbans, that were part of the Turkish national costume. Busbecq sent packets of seeds back to Vienna, and from there the flowers gradually began spreading around Europe—initially to the commercial cities, then to the market towns, and finally, like water finding its level, into every nook of the countryside.

At first the bulbs were such a novelty that many did not know what they were. The story is told of a merchant who received some as a present in a shipment of goods from Turkey. Believing them to be a strange variety of onions, he cooked and ate a few of them. But their flattish taste was definitely unappealing, even after he doused them with liberal portions of vinegar and condiments, so he planted them, hoping their flavor would improve in his soil, which he imagined was richer than that of his Turkish counterpart. One can well picture his surprise and unbounded delight when the "onions" blossomed into the most astonishing flowers he had ever seen!

Soon there was a raging fever, generated by the desire for the exotic bulbs which everyone wanted to brighten the landscape after winter's bleakness. Holland was especially susceptible to this fever, and the neat, flower-loving Dutch began converting the growing of tulips from a pleasure into a business. Everyone—noblemen, mechanics, farmers, even rag-pickers and chimney-sweeps—began raising tulips, each grower hoping he could come up with a new and improved strain which would bring a fantastic price. Normally conservative men developed an almost insane passion to possess the rarest types of tulips, and at the height of the epidemic, which has justly been called "tulipomania," one variety, regally named Semper Augustus, sold for nearly four thousand dollars—with a new carriage and two magnificent horses thrown in as extra payment! Other tulip bulbs sold for almost as much, although the purchaser, often more interested in speculation than in actually growing the strain, sometimes would never even see the bulb before he resold his rights to it for a higher price. Fabulous fortunes were made without the bulb's being taken from the ground. Homes and businesses were mortgaged as speculation grew rampant. And shady dealers appeared, with false guarantees of unique bulbs for which the world would clamor. When the bulbs bloomed the following spring, they turned out to be merely one of the common varieties, bringing ruin to the men who purchased them at exorbitant prices.

In France the situation was almost as frantic. No woman of fashion would be seen in the spring without a bouquet of tulips—and they had to be rare, if not absolutely unique—tucked provocatively into her low-cut frock. To meet this demand, French florists would pay unbelievable prices for rare strains. A grower could become rich overnight if he came up with a new breed. One brewer exchanged his flourishing brewery for a single bulb; and there was a young swain who took as his bride's dowry a lone tulip of rare vintage.

When the inevitable crash came in 1637, the dazed population began nursing their financial woes, hardly believing that such a craze could have possessed them. But the flower continued to be popular, and the Dutch, with their passion for beauty and their rich, damp fields, continued the care and nurture of the bulbs as a national business. They have maintained their leadership in the tulip trade ever since.

CHAPTER TEN

WHAT'S IN A NAME?

True and Apocryphal Stories

*N*ot only bulbs, but other flowering plants have interesting histories. Flowers were considered important even in the days of the early Egyptians. Most of these ancient gardeners preferred bachelor buttons, according to Richardson Wright in *The Story of Gardening*. But Cleopatra loved roses and even went so far as to cover her banquet floor a foot and a half deep with them. Later, when her guests retired, they found their beds fragrant with rose petals which had been used to stuff the mattresses. The hanging gardens of Babylon were famous throughout the ancient world, and the Persians, who took over the Babylonian empire, used gardens as a focal point around which they built their homes. The gardens were always separated from the arid landscape by high walls, and were frequently places of great splendor. The esteem in which the Persians held their gardens is indicated by their chief prophet, Zoroaster, who described heaven as a vast garden called "paradise." The Bible records a sumptuous party given in one of these Persian paradises:

> . . . the king made a feast unto all the people that were present in Shushan the palace, both great and small, seven days, in the court of the garden of the king's palace. There were hangings of white cloth, of green and of blue, fastened with cords of fine linen and purple to silver rings and pillars of marble: the couches were of gold and silver, upon a pavement of red, and white, and yellow, and black marble.

King Solomon shared this veneration for gardens. The magnificent plantings at his palace in Jerusalem had many prize irises and lilies;

and the Song of Solomon contains many verses alluding to the pleasure to be found in such gardens:

> Awake, O north wind; and come, thou south;
> Blow upon my garden, that the spices thereof may flow out.
> Let my beloved come into his garden,
> And eat his precious fruits.

Flowers played an important part in the everyday life of the ancient Greeks. Dozens of legends, some of which have already been related, grew up around the narcissus, the hyacinth, and other flowers. The commercially minded city of Corinth made a business of drying the rhizomes of rare iris plants and converting them into the fragrances highly valued by the Grecian ladies.

The Romans held the aster in special veneration, believing it sprouted from a tear of the star goddess, Astraea. After Christianity overthrew the old deities, Astraea was transformed into Virgo, the Virgin, and thereby continued to occupy her place among the constellations of the zodiac. The aster flowers, once under the spell of Astraea, continued to have magical charms, however, and according to Vernon Quinn in *Stories and Legends of Garden Flowers*, superstitious Europeans during the Dark Ages solemnly burned aster leaves to frighten serpents away.

After Rome sent her powerful legions into Britain, many new plants were introduced there: among them elms, walnuts, and Grecian irises. Yet England had its own distinctive vegetation: vast fields of white roses, which so impressed the tough legionaries that they called the island "Albion," which meant "the white place," and referred to the roses as well as the cliffs of Dover.

The English had many flowers that were believed to contain potent forces against sickness. They were convinced that the alyssum, which they called madwort, would prevent hydrophobia from the bite of a rabid dog. The hollyhock—which originated in distant China, made its way westward over dusty caravan routes, then reached England as part of the booty the Crusaders brought from the ravished Holy Land—was called "holy" from the place from which it had been carried, and "hock" from its supposed ability to cure a swelling in a man's heel, or hock. The phlox, which was unknown in Europe until it was imported from North America, was valued by the English as a charm against Satan. The Germans, however, preferred the primrose for this purpose.

Meanwhile other civilizations were thriving in the Orient. In China there was a sacred feeling about the garden not found in Europe. This veneration came largely as a result of the teachings of two great thinkers: Confucius, who insisted that a cultured man must know the Seven Arts—one of which was how to cultivate flowers; and Lao Tse, who believed that heaven was inhabited by eight immortals, one of whom was a gardener. Although the peony was king of the Chinese flowers (one magnificent garden was famous for its 60,000 plants), usually flowers did not figure conspicuously in the plantings. Instead, the Chinese landscape gardener tried to fill his space with miniature mountains, valleys, and rivers in a direct imitation of nature, which probably dated back to the most ancient days of Chinese culture.

The Japanese also valued a garden highly. Everything was personal to them in their landscaping: from each individual stone to the tiny bonsai trees. They, too, imitated nature, and there were no flowers, for they were considered too gross for this self-contained version of paradise. Nevertheless, flowers played an important part in Japanese life. According to an old legend, the chrysanthemum originated on the island and for over 1,000 years the flower has been the venerated emblem of the imperial ruler.

American gardening began when the Massachusetts Company shipped hollyhock, rose, and pink seeds to a land where they had never grown before. Later, other plants were imported: anemones, columbines, stock, primroses, and yellow daylilies.

But America had not been without its share of plants. Europeans had never tasted corn, pumpkins, squash, or tomatoes, nor had they smoked tobacco, until they came to the New World. They had never seen the towering sunflower, smelled the fragrance of honeysuckle, or known forest glens graced by dog-toothed violets. And they had never enjoyed that most magnificent of all trees, the autumnal sugar maple.

Many of the most brilliant of our flowers are Mexican. For example, there are the canna lilies, whose seeds were once used as rosary beads. Mexican, too, are the marigolds, whose bright yellow impressed Cortez and his adventurers on their fabulous march into the heartland of the Aztec empire. The Church officials who followed Cortez, determined to maintain their hold over the pagan Indians even in the smallest things, renamed the flower for the Virgin: "Mary's gold." All our marigolds, whether they are the French or African varieties, stem from the original Mexican stock.

Much more important to the Aztecs than the wild marigolds were the sturdy zinnias, renamed by the Swedish biologist Carolus Linnaeus for Johann Zinn, a friend who had just died—although it certainly would have been far more appropriate to have called it after Montezuma or some other Mexican leader. The Aztecs believed the flower had the power to insure a good corn crop, and so it was treated with great respect.

But the most sacred Aztec flower was the giant dahlia, which Linnaeus, again disregarding history, renamed for another friend, Andreas Dahl. Far more descriptive is the Aztec name, *acoctii*, which means war flower. Dull red in its natural state, like dried blood, it was the symbol of the war god, one of the chief deities of the aggressive Aztec nation. Periodically the Aztecs placed dahlias around a sacrificial stone dedicated to this god, then cut out the still-beating hearts of prisoners taken in battle!

The history of the petunia is less grim. Its name comes from the

Indian word for tobacco. European explorers found petunias growing wild along the banks of the Rio de la Plata in South America. However, this most popular summer flower was not introduced into Europe until 1823. The first blossoms were white only, but soon a rose-violet strain was discovered along the Uruguay River, and it is from these two varieties that all our current colors have been derived.

CHAPTER ELEVEN

OUT OF THE
MURKY DEPTHS

Evolution of Animals

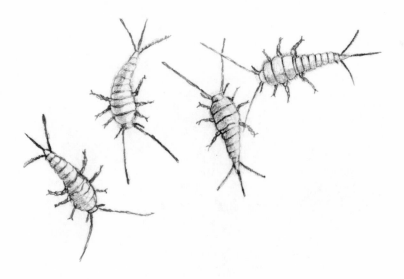

*O*n warm days of late spring I often kneel beside the small pond
I have dug near the willow at the far end of my yard to watch the
constant splattering of tiny bubbles which burst to the surface as the
algae shake oxygen out of the carbon dioxide dissolved in the water.
The evolution of the oxygen-consuming animals had to wait while the
plants enriched the atmosphere, bubble by bubble. To appreciate the
degree to which the animals are dependent on the plants it should be
noted that man and the rest of the animals would completely exhaust
the earth's oxygen in less than a year should the plants stop producing this vital gas!

How did it happen that the animals branched off from the plant
line? What need was there for animals? Plants had proved to be
masters of survival: they could reproduce by the millions, could adapt
themselves to changes in temperature, could exist in nearly boiling
water or on the barren rocks of wintry mountains.

Yet the emergence of animals was inevitable, for the early plant
organisms were not entirely passive. They reached out toward light,
grew toward food, and shied away from unfavorable elements. Their
sperm searched out the eggs and their fertilized eggs often swam
about until a suitable location was encountered. Viewed in this way,

there is not too great a step from the sedentary, emotionless world of the plants to the active, tense world of the animals. When enough oxygen had been produced, certain of the protozoa—such as the euglena—began adopting a new life pattern. They captured their food in a predatory manner. Around that portion of their bodies which moved toward the food, certain essential functions began to congregate, such as the primitive gullet, eye-spot, and antenna of the euglena.

Gradually some of these single-celled animals found they could capture more food by banding together. Of course this was not a conscious plan. It merely happened that those cells which so cooperated prospered—and their progeny also prospered. And so the next major advance in animal evolution occurred: the creation of the first many-celled animals.

Some of these early creatures are still found in ponds like mine. One day I noticed something I had not been aware of before. Protruding from the floor of the pond were wire-thin, darkish plants— or at least they seemed to be plants, for they gyrated gently in the water. And from the top of each were five arms, dancing slowly, almost majestically. I reached down toward them with a small stick, but when I touched one of them, the whole growth disappeared! I looked in wonder, but the thing had vanished.

What I had come upon was not a plant, but one of the earliest, most primitive animals: the hydra. As I continued to watch, I discovered that a touch will not cause a hydra really to disappear—it merely contracts from a half-inch long to a nubbin of less than a tenth this size. It gives me an eerie feeling to watch the menacing motions of the hydra—an animal from earliest time. In this primitive creature, already you can see the vicious character of the predator. Each of the tentacles contains poisonous arrows which are shot at the unsuspecting minutiae that float or swim by. Once the victim is helpless, the tentacles wrap around him and he is ushered into the mouth-opening.

The body of the common fresh-water hydra is only two cells thick: the external ones having specialized into a sort of skin, the interior ones assuming the digestive functions. Although the hydra is usually stationary like a plant, it can move when the occasion arises. Then watch it: the creature bends down until its mouth fastens onto the floor of the pond. This done, the base of the hydra pulls itself up to the mouth. Slowly, the weird animal moves—an automaton walking

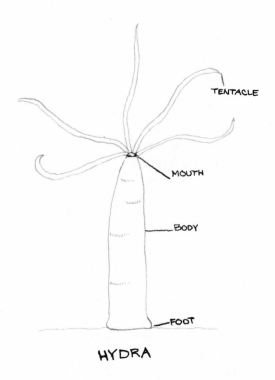

HYDRA

without a brain, without legs, without eyes, knowing only the vaguest sense of touch, and the insatiable hunger that drives all animals.

The warm Paleozoic sea still covered the earth when certain kinds of animals began evolving more complex organs—organs which enabled them to contend with their environment more effectively. Size was an asset, for larger animals were not so likely to be swept away by the currents, and they could roam farther in search of algae and other food. In addition, increased physical power came with size, and it wasn't long before the larger members of the newly created species began to prey upon those smaller than themselves.

The foremost requisite for increased size was a method of insuring that food and oxygen could be passed on to the inner cells. Two important innovations accomplished this. The first was blood, which carried oxygen and dissolved food. The second was a heart, a mass of specialized muscles which squeezed the blood out toward the innermost organs.

The development of blood and heart brought forth a grand proliferation of large-sized creatures—such as the ancestors of the octopus and the squid. Many of the new animals lived in massive shells. These shells, accumulating in vast numbers as the animals died, hardened and became the limestone bedrock which not only underlies my garden and most of the Midwest, but forms the massive abutment over which the waters tumble at Niagara.

A reminder of those Paleozoic days still exists in my pond. This is the humble snail. Although it may seem that the snail, and its land-based cousin, the garden slug (who along the way lost his shell) are not impressive, diagrams of their internal organs reveal just how far they have progressed from their hydra ancestors.

The snail has a heart, pulsating with life, as in man. The land species have lungs, too. Watch a snail closely and you can see him breathing: his throat is near the place where the shell meets the body. When he slides into the water, he calmly fills his lungs and uses them as gills! A snail's mouth is directly beneath his eye-stalks. He has jaws with strong muscles, and it is not difficult to watch them move as he feasts on algae and moss growing on the water lily leaves. The food goes down a slender throat, is further digested in a crop, passes into a rounded

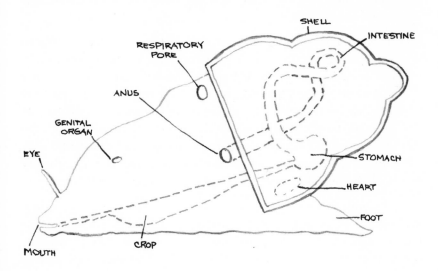

SNAIL

stomach, then circulates through a long, twisted intestine, where it is absorbed into the blood. The residue is ejected through a small hole beside the throat. This odd digestive tract, which turns back upon itself, is a result of the transformation of the snail's shell from a flat shape, like those of the clam, to a conical shape.

Strangely, it is quite possible to develop a degree of affection for the unassuming snail. Watch him climb up the slender stalk of a water lily. He has a liquid grace which should not be dismissed merely because snails are slower than fishes. Actually the progress of a snail is faster than we imagine. I once marked the shell of one and tossed him into the center of the pond. Three hours later the little creature poked his head out of the water. In this short time he had climbed through the forest of seaweed and lily stems and up the plastic pond side—a distance of about five feet.

Snails have well-developed eyes, complete with cornea, lens, and retina. A snail can see differences of light intensity, and thereby make out a watery blur of objects around him. When I hold one in my hand, he turns his eye-stalks toward me, aware of something, but not having a real brain, his movement is merely a reflex action.

Nevertheless, even though snails do not have brains, they are able to develop surprising attachments toward one another. Charles Darwin relates an example:

An accurate observer, Mr. Lonsdale, informs me that he placed a pair of land-snails ("Helix pomatia"), one of which was weakly, into a small and ill-provided garden. After a short time the strong and healthy individual disappeared, and was traced by its track of slime over a wall into an adjoining well-stocked garden. Mr. Lonsdale concluded that it had deserted its sickly mate; but after an absence of twenty-four hours it returned, and apparently communicated the result of its successful exploration, for both then started along the same track and disappeared over the wall.

Although Darwin speaks of the snail and his "mate," this is misleading, for there is no sex differentiation. Each has both male and female organs. I have seen two snails in a state of union: the male organ of each (which protrudes from his head region) implanted in the female opening, also in the head region. So tight is this mutual embrace that one snail is often lifted off its support. Later the snails will produce eggs in large, easily seen packets of foamy jelly along the side of the pond or attached to the aquatic plants.

The earthworm is higher in the evolutionary scale. It is difficult for us who have become accustomed to seeing it slithering out from a spadeful of dirt, to realize either the extreme complexity of the worm's body or the important place it occupies in the evolutionary pattern. Possibly the earthworm's most interesting innovation is that of body segmentation. By means of this segmentation he has been able to achieve a degree of specialization that is far superior to that of the animals beneath him in evolution.

Examine the sketch of the earthworm. In the first segment is the mouth. A small brain is located in the third segment and from this brain a nerve cord runs the entire length of the body—similar to the arrangement of our own nervous system. A throat extends from the mouth to the fifteenth segment, where an enlarged crop temporarily

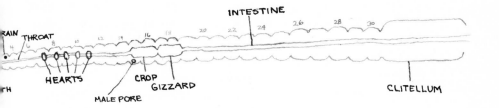

EARTHWORM

stores the vegetative matter. A thick-walled gizzard occupies segments seventeen and eighteen, and this organ, which grinds the food into tiny fragments by means of sand grains present there, takes the place of teeth. As the food passes into the intestine, which extends through the rest of the body (this total length may be as long as 180 segments) most of it is digested by means of enzymes secreted there. Finally, the undigested matter—sand, grains of dirt, humus and other organic matter—is ejected through the last segment in the form of the castings we see so often in small, black piles on the ground. These castings are extremely rich and are important in maintaining soil fertility.

Yet is is not necessary to dissect a worm to examine it. Simply dig one up, as I did. He was a fat, frisky thing, and once I got him washed off, his body glowed with a pleasing purplish iridescence. When I placed him in the palm of my hand, I felt the minute, spiked hairs with which he pushed himself forward, bristle against my skin like fine sandpaper.

The earthworm was amazingly active. Its long, tapered head nuzzled into the cracks between my fingers. Then he leaned far over the edge of my hand seeking his native soil. As he did so, the last ten segments flattened to almost twice their ordinary width, and the bristles turned so that they faced forward and braced his body. When he is in his burrow, these rear bristles make it impossible to pull him out.

Each time the worm stretched, I could see the network of blood vessels standing out red and vivid close to his skin. Worms have five pairs of hearts, located in segments seven to eleven, and as the hearts pulsated, the blood shot forward in dark ribbons.

The earthworm's reproductive system is complicated. As with the snails and most lower forms of life, an earthworm has both male and female organs. The male reproductive system can be seen as small slits standing out from the rest of segment fifteen and slightly lighter in color. Trailing backward from these pore openings are a series of small ridges which lead to the clitellum, a conspicuous swelling, usually beige in color, around segments thirty-one to thirty-seven.

On most warm, damp summer nights you can find the earthworms paired. To mate, they bring their underportions together. The clitellum of each grips segments seven to twelve of the other, with special spiked hairs actually penetrating the other's body. Sperm now pass along the ridges leading from the male pore, entering the other's female opening, which is inconspicuous in the fourteenth segment.

Soon after mating a cocoon forms over the clitellum. Up to twenty-eight eggs are deposited in this cocoon, which then moves upward along the worm's body. As it passes over segment fourteen, sperm from the mate, which had been stored in small sacs, flows into the cocoon fertilizing the eggs. Finally the cocoon moves over the worm's head, and remains in the earth until the young hatch in two weeks.

From the earthworm, evolution proceeded upward to the arthropods, next to the vertebrates (of which man is one) the highest form of life. The arthropods have three divisions: the crustaceans (such as crabs, shrimps, and crawfish), the spiders, and the multitudinous insects. The nervous system, eyes, and other sense organs of the arthropods are well-developed, giving them a quickness of response that contrasts sharply with the lethargic movements of the planaria, snails, and earthworms.

Of the three classes, the crustaceans are probably lowest in the evolutionary scale, for nearly all of them exist in a watery environment. The only crustacean found in the ordinary garden is the pill bug, that little armour-plated, many-legged animal who instantly rolls up into a pill-like ball when disturbed. The pill bugs have one startling characteristic—they have never lost their tie to the ancient ocean. Even though they are quite successful land animals, they still breathe by means of gills. For this reason they come out mainly during the evening moistness, spending the day safely ensconced in the humid air beneath rocks or pieces of wood.

The insects are divided into three general classifications. Most primitive are those which undergo no metamorphosis (radical change in body structure) between the young and the adult stages, and have not yet evolved wings. The silverfish, those common household pests, are thought to be the ancestors of all insects. Another are the spring-tails, or garden fleas, which although of minute size, make the puddles of my early May garden seem alive with their darting movements.

An easily observed representative of the second group, those that undergo partial metamorphosis, is the grasshopper. While there are five or six separate stages before the young nymph becomes an adult, at each stage the immature grasshopper is clearly a junior edition of the adult. As you look about your garden, you will recognize the baby nymph by his runty size. After he sheds his skin the first time, he is somewhat larger, with his abdomen now clearly visible and a pair of stubby growths called wing pads just in the process of forming. With each successive moult, the abdomen and wing pads grow, until the adult form is reached. At this point the wing pads become true wings and the insect is able to fly.

I recommended the grasshopper as an ideal specimen for observation of the insect species, for hoppers are quite large and thrive in captivity. Examine his head: you can discern the outlines of three segments, or somites, which show his ancient earthworm lineage. Behind the head is the thorax, where there are more fused somites.

The thorax contains three pairs of legs, each of which are equipped both with fleshy pads (whereby he clings to such objects as glass) and with claws for grasping rough places. If you rub your finger over these claws, you will be impressed by their sharpness.

The thorax also contains the wings. Insect wings are projections of the body covering. They are membranes only two cells thick and have nothing in common with the muscular legs. Thus, they are completely different from the relatively massive wings of birds, which have the same bony structure as their legs. Indeed, the insect wing, so frail yet so powerful, is one of the miracles of nature. If your hopper specimen dies, take off his wing and observe it under a magnifying glass. You will see a true work of art:

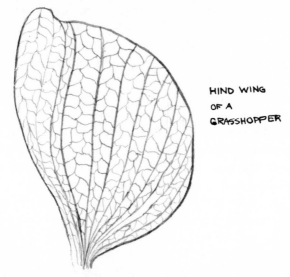

HIND WING
OF A
GRASSHOPPER

Behind the thorax is the abdomen. Notice the ten pairs of tiny, brownish holes, or spiracles, along the lower portion of the abdomen. When the hopper breathes, he opens the first four pairs and the air flows in and through his body by means of small tubes. (Since insect bodies are so small, they have no need for the more complex system of lungs buried deep within the body, and blood, red with hemoglobin, transporting oxygen to the cells far within. Actually, it is this air tube arrangement that restricts the size of insects.) At expiration, the hopper can be seen to close the first four spiracles and to open the rear six through which the air is ejected.

Superior to grasshoppers and other insects such as crickets, termites, dragonflies, aphids, and cicadas, whose young resemble the adult stage, are those insects that undergo true, or complete, metamorphosis. The most obvious example is the butterfly, whose caterpillar (or larva) youth bears absolutely no resemblance to the multi-hued splendor of the adult. In complete metamorphosis the larval form has no wings and spends nearly all its time eating and growing. Then, when it reaches its maximum size, it weaves a cocoon and, as a pupa, undergoes a thorough bodily rearrangement. After the proper time has elapsed, the adult emerges. His main function is reproduction and, because he has wings, he can travel far in search of a mate. Successful representatives of complete metamorphosis are bees, ants, houseflies, fireflies, and mosquitoes.

The metamorphosis of only *one* butterfly is fascinating, but metamorphosis in the mass is something else again. Early one spring I approached the pond and to my astonishment I found the water to be almost like jelly with countless thousands of mosquito larvae, called wigglers. They had been born from eggs of females who had hibernated all winter. The eggs had probably been laid just three days ago.

It was astonishing enough to see the tremendous profusion of life, but when I leaned over to get a better look, they all dived for the bottom—and the water writhed. They would soon be transformed into pupae and float helplessly near the surface and then the fish that I would hurriedly place in the pond would consume nearly their entire population. But some would survive, and, of course, some did.

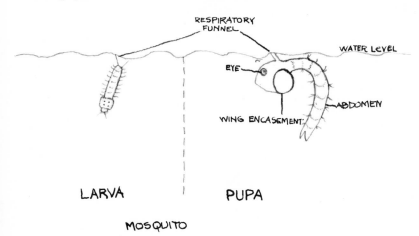

RESPIRATORY FUNNEL

WATER LEVEL

EYE

ABDOMEN

WING ENCASEMENT

LARVA   PUPA

MOSQUITO

CHAPTER TWELVE

DEEP SUMMER

*T*he seasons have personalities as distinct as those of human beings. Winter is a snowy day in early January when all is white and fresh without the dirt and dreariness of February. Spring is a balmy, laughing day in May fragrant with honeysuckle and the songs of warblers. Autumn is a period in mid-October, when the atmosphere is hazy with burning leaves, yet the scenery is still bright with the flaming maples and smoldering oaks.

The true personality of summer is reached during the languid days of August—so different from July when there is still the enthusiasm of early summer; so different from September with its whisper of autumn. In August there is a fullness in the torpid air. It is a time for relaxation and peace. It is a time for casual meals of potato salad and cold cuts topped off with chilled wedges of watermelon; a time for parties at the beach or for boat rides down a slow-moving river. It is a time for popsicles, lemonade, and outdoor concerts in the park, for vacations in the mountains. It is a time when sounds seem to carry farther: the laughter of children, the excited voice of a baseball announcer, the drowsy rumble of a power mower. It is a time for quiet, lazy afternoons.

I relax, content to let the earth turn, the flowers multiply, the clouds drift by. A breeze nuzzles me like a friendly, panting dog. Butterflies glide among the flowers and often land on my shoulder, making me feel that all living forms are closer together now that the fierce competition of early summer has given way to the bounty of August.

From out of the sky great cloud galleons sail toward my yard. These cumulus clouds are typical of summer and are quite different from any other clouds. Whereas many cloud formations are the result of a collision between a warm, wet upsurge from the south and a cold front from the north, the cumulus thunderheads are local events—they are, in a manner of speaking, our own personal clouds. Given a typical day of deep summer—the temperature high, the air sticky, with no breeze or at most a faint one from the south—thunderclouds are imminent. Such clouds are triggered by some local condition: usually by the prolonged contact of some slow-moving air with large areas of plowed fields or sunlit roofs which give off updrafts of heated air far greater than the nearby woodlands or prairies. This explains why there are few thunderstorms in the morning or in the winter. The fields and rooftops have to heat up first.

But once the process begins there is no stopping. It is like an explosion. While hot air ordinarily rises at a moderate rate which allows it to cool as it reaches the upper atmosphere, thunderclouds shoot skyward so rapidly they reach fantastic heights before cooling. The original updraft is only partially responsible for this phenomenon, for the incipient thundercloud feeds upon itself in a complex chain reaction which involves a tremendous increase in heat as mist forms from condensing water vapor. (A similar, though opposite, occurrence takes place when your hand is cooled by water evaporating from it.) As the cloud spumes higher and higher, more water condenses, thus generating even greater heat, and this heat enables the cloud to continue its billowing, turbulent ascent.

Those who have watched the growth of a thundercloud find it most impressive. In an incredibly short time—usually less than a half hour—the cloud soars into the blue, leaving the 1,600 foot height of the ordinary cumulus family far behind. Up, up it explodes, foaming and tumbling, a vertical cataract, a Niagara in reverse—two miles, four miles, perhaps even up to ten miles, or 52,800 feet! This fantastic jet of water has ripped many a plane apart, for its vicious cross-currents sometimes reach a speed of 160 miles per hour. Guy Murchie in *The Song of the Sky* tells of a glider pilot caught in a thundercloud upsweep watching helplessly as his altimeter went "round like the hands of a crazy clock," and all the while rain lashed about him and thunder roared in terrifying blasts.

But thunderclouds do more than provide us with summer spectacles and an occasional drenching. They thrive on the high humidity

which makes some of our deep summer days oppressive. Like benefi-
cent leviathans, they gobble up this moisture, then send it pelting to
earth, leaving the air drier and the fields and gardens wetter—a most
salubrious arrangement. In addition, lightning produces a consider-
able amount of nitrogen fertilizer—up to 100 million tons a year,
according to George Kimbel and Raymond Bush in *The Weather.*

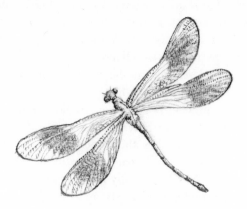

Most of the events of deep summer are not so dramatic. I had
a friend for about a week, a ten-spot dragonfly who perched on the
tip of a stick I used to prop up a nicotiana plant. The dragonfly was a
proud, fearless insect, who regarded me suspiciously with his large,
rotating eyes. But once he determined I meant him no harm, he was
content to share the location with me for hours on end.

He was a beautiful creature. His wings were long as he spread them
full in the dancing, willow-made shadows. They were transparent with
a slightly bluish tint, except for the conspicuous white spots which
stood out on each of the two pairs of wings. His large head was black
and round as a ballbearing. He held on to his perch by wrapping his
long, delicate legs around the stick, while his thin, dark abdomen,
which has given him the name of darning needle (but which is actually quite harmless), made a neat 45-degree angle with the rest of his
body. When I moved closer, I could see his abdomen expanding and
contracting for dragonflies breathe through tiny holes in the abdomen
as all insects do. Every so often he would sight some object flying
nearby and he would zoom off in hot pursuit, his wings whirring
loudly.

Dragonflies are among the most primitive insects. Having evolved during the steamy age of the coal ferns and giant club mosses, they grew to great size, their wingspan often reaching two-and-a-half feet. They were the very first monarchs of the sky, dominating the airways 200 million years before the advent of either the birds or the bees, and more than 300 million years before man began sending his rigid projectiles into the blue. Other insects that developed during those ancient days had similar types of wings which could not fold back, but this proved such a hindrance in flying though the dense forests that they eventually died out. However, the dragonflies, although fierce competitors, adapted by growing smaller and today they exist in much the same form (except for size) as when they first appeared.

The dragonflies show their early evolutionary form in other ways, too. Nearly 85 per cent of all insects go through a complete metamorphosis similar to the caterpillar-cocoon-adult stages of the moth. This is a great advantage, for it represents the ultimate in specialization: the caterpillar is able to gorge himself on green food, while the adult with wings and little appetite is able to seek out a mate. But the dragonflies never reached this complex stage of development. They spend their youth as aquatic nymphs and when the hour of adulthood arrives, the nymph simply climbs to the surface, sheds its skin (which you may find hanging to the stalk of a waterplant) and emerges, without a cocoon phase or change in basic structure, as a full-grown adult.

Darwin called dragonflies "the tyrants of the insect-world." With their powerful wings they can fly forward up to 60 miles per hour, and they can also hover quite stationary by using their abdomen as a rudder. In addition, they can even fly backward, a feat which, according to Harold Bastin in *Freaks and Marvels of Insect Life*, makes them the most accomplished of all insect aeronauts. This skill at flying and maneuvering is the main reason for their survival for their food is mainly insects, such as mosquitoes, stabbed by barbs on the dragonflies' legs as they are flying. If you look closely, you can see these barbs.

The mating of most animals is rarely witnessed. Yet the brazen dragonflies perform their acts of reproduction openly. Who has not seen the paired insects flying though the summer air? When the act is completed, the female will swoop over a pond dipping her abdomen as she lays her eggs in the water.

Butterflies in a dazzling and never-ending array also come to my deep summer garden. There are the ever-present cabbage butterflies with bright white wings, a small black spot on each one. Although they are exceedingly common through the Midwest, they are actually European immigrants who arrived in this country only about a hundred years ago. The sulfurs are present too, yellow creatures who love clover as much as honeybees do. When the sulfurs eat, they stand on the very tip of the flower petals, then uncurl their tongues (which seem to be even longer than their legs) so that they easily penetrate the nectar-rich chambers of the blossom heart. They do not have the hard work of climbing through the dense petals that characterizes the stubby-tongued bee.

Fritillaries and painted ladies often wandered through my flower-beds, their brownish wings spotted with blacks, oranges, whites, tans, or pale yellows. Red admirals appeared frequently too, their flashing scarlet bands across black wings making them conspicuous wherever they went. Although the swallowtails (with their lustrous bluish-black wings ending in the graceful, swallow-like sweep which gives them their name) are spectacular, the monarchs, sporting bright orange wings netted in black, are nearly as beautiful. Viceroys are usually near the monarchs, and are so like them (except that the viceroys are smaller and their black markings are darker) that they have become the classic example of survival by mimicry. Birds cannot distinguish the savory viceroy from the bad-tasting monarchs—and so they leave both alone.

For several weeks each summer a mourning cloak flutters about, his dark wings set off by a distinct band of yellow on the outer portions. He wanders through my garden, sails over the hedge to my neighbor's yard, then suddenly reappears. What a pleasure it is to see him glide high in the tepid air, graceful as a wind-borne piece of tinsel. Along with the dragonfly, he is usually my closest deep summer companion.

Yet for one day it was not the mourning cloak, but a frisky comma butterfly which occupied most of my attention. Although his appearance was hardly eye-catching (not overly bright brownish wings, polka-dotted with black, and arching inward in the form of a comma), he sat at my feet luxuriating in the sun for most of the day. After I went indoors toward the end of the afternoon, I thought I had seen the

last of him. But when the family was having dinner on the patio, he began flapping around our lamb chops just as if he were a pet waiting to be fed. The next morning he was gone, and I have not seen a comma in my neighborhood since.

Butterflies generally live only about six weeks—the same life span as that of the honeybee. But theirs is a carefree existence. Donald Culross Peattie in *A Cup of Sky* reminds us that the butterflies have always been symbols of frivolity and that they toil no more than is absolutely necessary to keep body and wing together. Their wing stroke is leisurely, only twelve times a second, compared with 250 times a second for the madly scurrying honeybee. It is a curious fact that their wings are actually colorless; the hues coming from minute scales attached to the wings so lightly that they rub off as "butterfly dust." Yet this bright coloration is essential, for the flashing wings not only attract potential mates but also confuse marauding birds who would otherwise attack the insect's tender body. And a ripped wing —even if more than half is gone—does not usually keep a butterfly from resuming his flight once the attacker has departed.

The derivation of the butterfly's brilliant colors challenged the mind of Darwin, who devoted an entire chapter to the subject in *The*

Descent of Man. Darwin's investigations showed that males greatly exceed females—nature's provision for the fertilization of each female. A male will mate with any willing female, but the female is far more choosy, making it necessary for the male to woo her. Often Darwin watched a group of males pirouetting around a female in a ritual dance. The female, possibly conditioned by the vivid flowers containing her food, usually chose the male with the brightest coloration. This meant, of course, that the characteristic of bright coloration was basic for mating and survival.

But, while the life of the adult butterfly is all nectar and roses, it was not like this in the beginning. He was born from a tiny egg, often barrel-shaped, laid on a twig. From this egg the caterpillar broke out into a hostile world. He was a helpless creature with a mouth made for chewing, not for defense. His body was tender and succulent, a juicy dish for the legions of insects and birds who sought him out. If the attack was outright and death was quick, the caterpillar was lucky. However, many times flies and wasps lay eggs on or within a caterpillar's body, and then the poor doomed creature has to live a tortured life while the grubs literally eat him alive. There is a remarkable picture in *Life's* Nature Library book *The Insects*, showing a still-living caterpillar whose body serves as the home for five large grubs and this can be clearly seen through the skin. I have often found caterpillars whose backs were studded with half a dozen or more grubs. These grubs grow quite rapidly by sucking the life juices from the captive caterpillar. Yet he is unable to shake them off. Only gradually does he shrivel up and die.

Once the caterpillar has grown to the proper size, he abandons his eating stage to transform himself into a chrysalis, which corresponds to a moth's cocoon, but has no silk around it. Although the chrysalises come in various shapes and colors (that of the monarch, for example, is like an oblong, turquoise jar with a lid on it) most are of a metallic-golden hue, from which the Greek word *chrysalis* is derived. Throughout the summer I find many of these pupal cases deposited around the yard—amid leaves, pasted to the side of my house, even on the bare pavement of my driveway.

One of my best studies was watching a large, green caterpillar turn from a vigorous, searching creature into a quiescent chrysalis. I brought the caterpillar into my house one afternoon and put him into an empty ten-gallon fish tank. I gave him a handful of leaves and let him gorge himself.

For three days he continued his voracious eating. Then, on the fourth day, he suddenly stopped eating and simply "rested" among the leaves. On the fifth day he began burrowing into the soil which I had placed on the tank bottom to a depth of three inches. He was very restless, butting his way through the loosely packed dirt with such force that I could follow him merely by watching the dirt rise. The following day he continued his burrowing as if he were instinctively searching for something.

The morning of the seventh day all was quiet. By holding the glass tank up, I found that he had butted out a neat and spacious chamber several times larger than himself. He lay partly curled in the chamber, seemingly dead. After waiting several days to see if anything would happen, I removed the dirt from the top, partially exposing the chamber. I touched him lightly and he jerked in a stiff, almost convulsive manner.

Checking on the caterpillar the next two mornings, I could find no change. With his once-fine green skin covered with dirt, his body motionless and rigid, and his interest in food entirely gone, I thought he would soon be dead.

But then the miracle happened. When I looked at him on the evening of the tenth day—the caterpillar was gone—and in its place was a chrysalis! The dirty skin of his former life lay crumpled at one side of the chamber. But the chrysalis was clean and bright and new. The lower portion was golden brown, like a freshly cooked waffle. The upper portion was still wet (so recently had the insect shed its skin) and it had a beautiful chartreuse luster. An hour later the luster was gone and the chrysalis took on its permanent dull copper color.

It is an interesting experience to hold a chrysalis in your hand. It feels cool, and it is slippery, but not greasy. It is rather hard, and there is absolutely no hint that anything alive exists inside. Even so, you can make out the general outline of the winged beauty that will soon appear. Four or five segments of the abdomen are obvious at the bottom; above them are the curved wrappings that shield the developing wings; and at the top are the encasements for the antennae and the head. Squeeze the chrysalis gently and you will feel it squirm. Yes, even though the animal is undergoing such a complete altera-

117

tion that at times the body is little more than a thick soup, it is alive.

At last the day comes when the chrysalis splits and the newly created butterfly crawls shakily out. He clings to a twig while he pumps fluid into his limp wings. They expand to such dimensions that they are often four times as large as the chrysalis which once covered them! As they harden, the butterfly flexes them, testing the air currents. Then suddenly he skims off into the summer afternoon, adding color to the beauty of the season.

The wonders of a deep summer day continue while the afternoon moves on. As the cicadas utter their shrill calls, I remember a Fabre experiment. He set off the village cannon beneath a tree full of cicadas, and the noisy little insects continued their outbursts—for the odd reason that they cannot hear!

Now the shadows gather, and the air begins to shimmer with circling groups of midges. Their swarming is in reality a love dance, since they mate on the wing. The sun hovers briefly on the horizon, drenching the landscape with amber light, exposing a maze of silken threads which covers the grass. These are really thousands of baby spiders which landed in my small meadow after sailing through the air (sometimes for long distances) by means of the long loop of silk which buoyed them up.

At last the day is over. Yet a night in deep summer is also saturated with life. The chirp of the crickets replaces the rasp of the cicadas, and the glinting fireflies and eerie, large-winged moths replace the dragonflies and butterflies. The air is still hot. I can feel it radiating from the cement blocks of the patio. I cross my legs and sit quietly.

CHAPTER THIRTEEN

AFTER TWILIGHT

Fireflies and Crickets

*A*lthough the hours of daylight are good, with rewarding hours of work and play, there is an entirely different mood in the evening, when the air seems hushed, and the creatures of the night come out of their secret hiding places.

The fireflies are the first to capture my attention and I find them enchanting. They take me back to my childhood when all things were new and mysterious. I remember the first time I ran among the swirling, flashing insects, cupping one in my hands when I caught him—fearful of his fire, yet curious to see him glow. Then the round abdomen lighted up with an amber brightness from which I could count the beads of perspiration in my grubby palms. And wonder of wonders, there was no burning in the fire, not even a perceptible warmth!

One of the mystifying characteristics of the firefly is that there is no fire in his glow, no incandescent flame that scorches and consumes, that feeds destructively upon itself. Whereas an electric light bulb wastes 70 percent of its energy in the form of heat rather than light, the firefly is able to produce its glow with only a 2 percent loss in heat. This humble insect is able to produce cool light—something that man with all his scientific advancement has never been able to achieve.

A common misconception about the firefly is that he is a fly. But anyone who has captured the slow-moving little bug will realize that he is not a true fly, for his outer wings are hard, not supple like those of a fly. Actually the firefly is a member of the beetle family. Like all beetles, they spend much of their lives as grubs burrowing through the dark earth. Although the adults are harmless (they eat neither plants nor animals during their brief above-the-ground-life), as larval grubs they prey upon snails, slugs, and earthworms. To kill, they sink fangs into their victims, through which first an anesthetic poison flows, then a serum that liquefies the body tissues. The vicious, wormlike grub pursues the life of a relentless hunter for two years. Then comes the metamorphosis and it changes into the harmless lantern-bearer that makes our summer nights so pleasant.

The firefly's bright glow, as with bird song, is not common to both sexes. It is the male who lights up most brilliantly; the female is usually just a sedentary bug—sometimes without wings—who twinkles back with a feeble glow. But it is enough. Mating is the sole purpose of their brief existence as adults, and once the eggs are deposited in the earth, the lives of the adults are over.

Another night-time inhabitant, the moth, is not as favorably regarded by humans as the firefly. It is true that moths are often pests: those that damage carpets and clothing, as well as the notorious peach and corn borers, the codling worm often found inside apples, the cutworms who topple many a highly prized garden plant, and the tent and webworms whose silken communities disfigure our trees—all caterpillar forms of moths. Even the relatively harmless millers who spiral around our lights leave us with a disagreeable image of the moth family.

Yet there are moths whose beauty must be seen to be believed. Take, for example, the luna moth, described by John Burroughs:

> At this time, behind and above me, concealed by a vase fern, reposed that lovely creature of the twilight, the luna moth, just out of her chrysalis, drying and inflating her wings. I chanced to lift the fern screen, and there was this marvel! Her body was as white and spotless as the snow, and her wings, with their Nile-green hue, as fair and delicate as—well, as only those of a luna moth can be. It is as immaculate as an angel. With a twig I carefully lifted her to the trunk of a maple sapling, where she clung and where I soon left her for the night.

Other large moths are equally beautiful. There is the promethea family: the female brownish, the male maroon, with amber fringes on their wings and a dark eyespot at the upper tips. There is the polyphemus clan: huge, tawny-colored moths, named for the violent, yet pathetic, giant of the *Odyssey*, the large spot on each of the rear wings representing his single eye. And there is the cecropia group—grandest of all, whose velvety five-and-a-half inch wings are rich

Luna

Crecopia

blackish-brown lined with carmine, white, and amber and are orna-
mented with four pale, cuneiform-shaped spots. Their bodies are furry
white with broken bands of fawn-tinted orange. Their heads are
graced with long, black antennae feathered with many radiating
sensory hairs.

Moths differ from butterflies in many respects. The most obvious
difference is that they are night-flyers. Almost as obvious is their
method of holding their wings while resting—moths spread their wings
flat, as flies and most other insects do, while butterflies bring their
wings close together, presumably so that daylight predators cannot
spot them too easily. In addition and more interestingly, the colors of
butterflies are illusory, for they are due to the refraction of light from
the minute scales which make up their wings, whereas the colors of
moths are due to actual pigments which are necessary because there
is no sunlight during the time of their activity. And that explains why

the moths' coloration fades so much more rapidly than the butterflies' when exposed to the bleaching effects of sunlight. The moths' antennae are far more intricate than the butterflies' which are usually simple structures resembling their legs. The complex form of the moths' antennae is probably due to the necessity of picking up the scent of members of the opposite sex when darkness precludes visual detection. And this leads to more of Henri Fabre's experiments.

The little man had carried home a great peacock cocoon from one of his rambles through the countryside, and early one morning the moth, an insect similar to our cecropia moth, emerged. He placed her, still damp with her pupal fluid, in a large bell-jar secured with screening at the top. He had no particular plans for her, and little did he realize that he was soon to be involved in a series of experiments which would extend over the next three years.

At about nine o'clock that evening, just as he was preparing for bed, his little son Paul rushed up to him, so excited that he had knocked over a chair. "Come and see these moths, big as birds! The room is full of them!" he screamed delightedly. In the kitchen Fabre found the bewildered cook waving her apron at the circling, large-winged moths, whom she mistook at first for bats. Hurrying on to the study, a disheveled room cluttered with his numerous experiments, Fabre and his son came upon an amazing sight:

> We enter the room, candle in hand. What we see is unforgettable. With a soft flick-flack the great moths fly around the bell-jar, alight, set off again, come back, fly up to the ceiling and down. They rush at the candle, putting it out with a stroke of their wings; they descend on our shoulders, clinging to our clothes, grazing our faces. The scene suggests a wizard's cave. . . .

Before the evening was over, the astonished Frenchman found that forty lovers had come to woo the virgin moth who was born only that morning. To get there they had to fly for many miles, then navigate through the maze of linden trees and lilac bushes which surrounded the run-down country house. They arrived in the black of night, yet there was not a scratch on them. Yes, it was most surprising.

Now Fabre's appetite was whetted. He could no more abandon his observations of the moth than could Audubon (for whom Fabre expressed a great admiration) resist tracking his birds throughout

North America. How had these forty male moths found his newly born female? From arduous searching throughout his neighborhood he knew how rare the great peacock cocoons were. He felt it must be the delicately shaped antennae which were able to pick up the female scent—a scent which he himself could not detect even though he was quite close to her. Therefore he clipped off the antennae of the moths who still flew about. Out of the sixteen, not a single one returned the next night—although the house was swarming with other ardent males. It was interesting, but not conclusive, for the males ordinarily lived only three days and perhaps all his moths may have died.

So the next night he drenched the room in which his female resided with naphthalene. If the moths actually located the female by her scent, might not the powerful odor confuse them? One wonders what his wife thought as he wrote: "I have only to stand in the doorway of the room to get a distinct smell of gasworks." Yet the artifice failed, for the moths went right to the female despite Fabre's manmade odor.

His curious mind was bubbling with more experiments, but on the ninth day his female laid her unfertilized eggs and died. That summer Fabre passed the word to the village urchins that he was in the market for great peacock caterpillars. He obtained a few females, watched them carefully over the winter, hovered over them as they came out of their cocoons; then suffered the disappointment of a frigid, blustery spell during the short time when the mating must occur. No males were able to conquer the weather and an entire year was lost.

That fall he and his urchins took to the fields and rounded up more cocoons. He waited anxiously over the winter, and when warm weather came and his female emerged, he was rewarded with a renewal of the evenings he had experienced two years earlier with the wooing male moths.

He had to know: was it actually the female's scent which enabled the gallants to find her? He still could hardly believe the males were actually able to detect the faint odor in the vastness of the freely circulating air. Yet when he placed the female in a jar hermetically sealed so no odor could escape, no males arrived.

To be absolutely sure that his theory was correct he had to rule out other possibilities. Could the moth be transmitting waves of some sort similar to the wireless telegraphy then being discussed with so much wonder? Had the glass somehow cut off these waves? He replaced the airtight seal with cotton and watched as the shadows lengthened. Would the hordes of male moths appear at their mating hour?

They came, filling the old house with the dusky beauty of their maroon and white, led there solely by the wondrous perfume of the female and the even more wondrous scent-receptivity of the feathered male antennae. Although Fabre was still not completely convinced, and even considered a fourth year of experiments, modern science has since proved the uncanny ability of moths to locate one another by their scents. Indeed, Fabre's estimate limiting reception to a mile and a half was conservative, for it is now known that moths can follow a faint perfume trail that radiates within nine square miles of them!

Sometimes, when I am awed by the stupendous powers of the insect world, I find myself sharing the nightmare of science fiction writers who fantasize a horrible Armageddon with insects the size of man. I imagine myself confronted by an angry ant powerful enough to lift a truck, whose scimitar pincers can easily pierce steel; or I imagine a firefly larva lashing out at me with fangs as thick as elephant tusks; or I fancy I am about to be caught by a dragonfly whose wings are as large as those of an airplane and upon whose terrible legs, bristling with spikes the size of swords, are the impaled remains of half a dozen unfortunate humans.

In this horrible fantasy, I see our farmlands infested with millions of giant caterpillars roaming over the fields like huge vacuum cleaners devouring 46,000 times their weight in a single day. How, I ask myself, could we fight against the proliferating aphids, when a single one could flood the world with 400 billion progeny at the end of a single year, each the size of a bloated beer keg? And what use would our air force be against bees that could change direction almost instantly, and were backed up by innumerable queen-factories each capable of producing 5,000 new bees every day!

In the dark night, these fears seem almost reasonable, but with daylight I am reassured. I know that it is physically impossible for any insect to grow beyond a certain maximum—already reached in most species—because (as already stated) they breathe by means of microscopic air tubes through which the air is diffused throughout their tiny bodies. But, since air can be diffused over only very short distances, animals with thicker bodies require internal lungs and a blood system with hemoglobin to transport oxygen. Insects lack this structure. It is as simple as that.

By the light of the moon I see a katydid walking slowly along the fence behind the honeysuckle. He is a shade of green which almost exactly matches the shrubbery; but more than that, his wings (folded back over his body) are almost identical to a pair of leaves, from their tapered shape to their finely etched vein lines. Certainly this insect is one of nature's most perfect camouflage jobs. Yet he is an ungraceful creature, with oversized antennae which are nearly as long as his body. When I touch one, he draws it back as though unhappy that anyone has dared to penetrate his masterful disguise.

I wait for him to begin his staccato song, only to find that "he" is a "she"—and it is only the male katydids that sing. But soon the night is filled with the call of courting katydids and although I do not see the males, in a few weeks I know I will find a clutch of minute, brownish eggs on some willow leaves nearby, no doubt left by the female katydid I now observe in the moonlight.

The katydids are soon joined and outsung by the crickets. Probably there is no combination of sounds more pleasing to the human ear over a long period of time than those made by the cricket. One can tire of the insistent twitter of the song sparrow, but never of the cricket's singing, for he brings a sense of tranquillity. His is a love song, just as with birds, and only the males sing—a fact which Darwin attributed to sexual selection. The first cricket chirps, Darwin believed, were made accidentally and when they proved pleasing to the less numerous females, the possessors of the chirp were insured a favorable response to their mating overtures.

A cricket makes his chirp by rubbing his wings together—wings which are nearly as tough as metal plates (as you can see for yourself by examining one of the numerous easily captured insects). These wings have on their undersides a heavy vein and on the upper portion a sharp ridge. As the insect moves one wing over the other, the ridge scrapes against the vein, producing a chirping sound. Although either wing may be scraped against the other, for some inexplicable reason almost all crickets carry the right wing over the left. Fabre, with his deep research into insect life, placed the left wing over the right at a time when they were still soft in the newly emerged nymph (for crickets are among the more primitive insects who do not undergo complete metamorphosis). Three days later the cricket began to play, and his instinct being even stronger than Fabre's will, he wrenched his wings back to their original position. "Your sorry science," Fabre scolds himself, "tried to make a left-handed player of him. He laughs at your devices and settles down to be right-handed for the rest of his life."

The chirp of the "little creaker" (which is what the original French word for cricket means) varies with the warmth of the night—so much so that one can pretty well estimate the temperature by counting the number of chirps per minute. Below 50 degrees Fahrenheit there will be only 50 chirps per minute; as the temperature rises, the rapidity of chirps increases so that by the time it is 80 or 85 degrees, the little fellow is fiddling at a frantic rate of well over 200 times a minute!

Yet with all his energetic rasping, the cricket is making sounds of remarkable subtlety. Recordings made by the American Museum of Natural History have indicated that cricket music consists of a series of artfully performed slurs such as an expert violinist delights in producing.

A night in deep summer is filled with many other creatures. Orb spiders weave the marvelously intricate nets which Peattie calls "the most complex structure built by any living creature save man himself." A daddy longlegs sprints across the patio—a harmless animal even

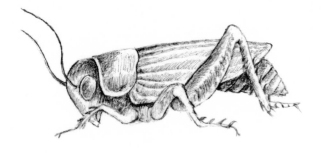

though he is related to the crab and scorpion. Earthworms pull themselves up from their dark tunnels to eat and to mate in the obscurity they crave. Slugs and pill bugs glide over the dewy ground, searching out damp, secluded feeding areas where they will be safe from tomorrow's sun. Stag beetles scramble over clumps of earth, their giant, virtually useless claws flashing to attract the females. The goldfish are sleeping even though their eyes are opened and I rub their shiny orange backs as they snooze close to the surface.

I recline on a chaise longue, close my eyes, and breathe in the fragrance of the purple and pink phlox which form the southern border of my miniature world. I experience deep contentment.

CHAPTER FOURTEEN

THE GOLDEN CITY

Bees and Wasps

I am not the only civilized creature in my backyard world. The bees are there, too. As soon as the wind carries the fragrance of April's first flowers, there is a murmur of excitement within the golden city, that honey-combed hollow in a nearby oak tree. The fanners begin to flex their muscles, for they must keep the city cool. At the city's gate the burly sentries gather, ready to repel any invaders. Hundreds of young nurses climb high in the amber combs, their thoughts on the infants they must tend. The foragers hurry to the take-off area and soar away by the hundreds. They know exactly where to fly, for located in their supple antennae are 5,000 scent-hollows which enable them to detect the perfume of a single blossom a half-mile distant.

A bee flits close by my head to make a six-point landing atop a large blossom. I put down my work and walk over to where she is already jabbing her long tongue into the inner recesses of the flower. What a delectable experience it must be to have 5,000 scent receptors and be immersed in the perfume of a flower!

As the bee leans far into the blossom, she brushes past the stamens, whose pollen granules are caught in her hairs; at the same time, she deposits some of the pollen contacted from other blossoms on the sticky tip of the pistil. Now she drinks the nectar by means of the tiny spoon at the end of her tongue. Back and forth she dips her tongue, rapidly, but not so quickly you cannot see her. The nectar flows down her throat, but does not pass into her digestive system. Instead, almost the entire amount is stored in a community "honey-stomach," an unusual sac where it will remain until she returns to the golden city. This honey-stomach can hold the nectar from more than 1,000 florets of clover, yet the bee must fill it sixty times before she contributes a single thimbleful of honey to the hive. To do this she will labor from dawn to dusk at such a ferocious pace that she will exhaust her vitality and die within four to six weeks.

Once the forager returns to the hive, there is still a great deal of work to be done before the nectar is changed into honey. First she empties the contents of her honey-stomach into the mouths of younger bees. These bees move the nectar back and forth across their tongues to evaporate some of the water. Next, to concentrate the nectar still more, it is placed into special open storage cells where constant fanning and certain chemicals from the worker's stomach convert the thin nectar into thick honey. After this happens, the cell is sealed with a cap of wax, and there the honey remains, like stored sunlight, until the seal is broken open to feed a hungry larva.

The average hive will need at least five hundred pounds of honey to carry it over the winter. Frank S. Stuart in his colorfully written book, *City of the Bees*, estimates that in an active hive, bees will have to visit 200 million blossoms to collect this much nectar—which suggests the degree to which bees pollinate the flowers.

We outsiders, who see the worker bees only when they come to our gardens, can hardly appreciate the stupendous achievement of this insect species. These small creatures have been able to erect a truly civilized, stable city thousands of years ahead of our own haphazard and ill-planned population centers. For a fascinating look at the intricate life inside the hive we can consult the work of Maurice Maeterlinck, who devoted twenty years to his *Life of the Bee*, which has become the classic in bee literature since its publication in 1901. Maeterlinck, who was also a prominent philosopher and playwright (he won the Nobel Prize for literature in 1911) found in his investigations of the bees something of man's own place in the natural world. "The most trivial secret of the non-human object we behold in nature," he wrote, "connects more closely perhaps with the profound enigma of our origin and our end than the secret of those of our passions that we study the most eagerly and the most passionately."

The soul of the golden city is the queen. Should the queen die, the colony begins to fall apart. Nurses no longer care for the young; sentries no longer guard the sacred portals; and the hard-working foragers wander disconsolately around the city, no longer visiting the flowers that yesterday held such fascination for them. The queen is different from her subjects. Her body is about twice as large and her abdomen is tapered at the end so that she may deposit her eggs within the narrow cell. It is this egg-laying capacity that makes the queen so essential, for she is the sole means by which the colony reproduces. In early spring, when the colony first awakens from its winter hibernation, she begins laying a half dozen eggs daily. As the hive begins to renew its strength, she increases her activity until during the bountiful clover season she is producing 2,000 eggs a day—sometimes as many as 5,000 under special conditions! The population of the golden city will rise until the queen is surrounded with up to 80,000 of her own progeny.

During the height of summer the hive will be in a state of feverish activity. The hive architects can scarcely construct cells fast enough to keep up with the queen, since she continues depositing eggs day and night—even while she is sleeping! These ingeniously constructed hexagonal cells (the erection of which Darwin called "the most wonderful of all known instincts") begin reaching down from the hollowed oak galleries in ever larger combs: flat, tongue-shaped, in layers of two cells slightly slanted upward at about 4 degrees. Honey is stored in the higher cells while larvae develop in the lower ones. As the colony expands, more combs are added, but the bees always allow ample avenues between each comb for the passage of the nurses.

The queen, who carries within her body up to 25 million sperm, can determine the sex of the egg by controlling the flow of the sperm: those which are fertilized develop into female workers, the others become male drones.

However, the queen is not the real ruler of the golden city. Rather it is some vague but omnipotent principle which Maeterlinck calls "the spirit of the hive." "It regulates day by day the number of births, and contrives that these shall strictly accord with the number of flowers that brighten the countryside." More than that, the spirit of the hive actually decrees that the unwilling queen must lay the eggs which will develop into rival queens, and that the workers, who normally submit to all her wishes, will protect these royal eggs from their sovereign, whose desire is to sting her rivals to death.

Then there comes the day when the first of the princesses is ready to leave her cell. Although the old queen is enraged, she is helpless, and when at last she realizes that the will of the hive is above hers, she prepares to leave the home in which she was for so long the absolute mistress. Somehow a mysterious boundary has been passed. The amber combs full of honey, the thousands of maturing young, the security of the old oak—all these have suddenly become part of an irretrievable past.

As she makes ready to leave, there is an unmistakable murmur within the golden city. Everything is in a state of confusion. A division forms between the majority of the workers who will follow their queen and those who will remain with the princess. Out of the golden city the loyalists pour—perhaps 50,000 of them, the old queen in their midst. They swarm to a nearby tree limb while scouts scatter in all directions to seek out a favorable location for a new hive. Professional beekeepers know that these swarming bees are in a strange, almost hypnotic condition—that the swarm may be gathered up in one's hands and deposited unprotestingly in a new apiary.

But in the natural state the swarm awaits the reports of the scouts. As each one returns, she conveys her information to the others. How do they do this? Peter Farb in *The Insects* (part of *Life's* Nature Library) states that the scouts do a dance which communicates their enthusiasm for the new site—the better the site, the greater their enthusiasm. After the reports of all sites have been given (Farb reports that 21 were being considered during his particular observation), the bees chose what they believed to be the best, then the swarm took off for the new location.

This is a perilous hour for the swarm. Before leaving the hive, they had gorged themselves with a six days' supply of honey. By taking up to four days to decide on a new site, they now have only two days left in which to settle down and begin the collection of more nectar. In addition, while flying to the new nest, they are exposed to the elements. Should wind or rain or a summer storm scatter them, all is lost. Teale, in *North with the Spring*, describes the pathetic sight of a lake strewn with the bodies of what had once been a bee swarm but which had been caught in a strong wind and deposited in the middle of the water.

Meanwhile, back in the old hive the situation is just as precarious. Before the young queen can begin laying, she must mate. To prevent inbreeding, the spirit of the hive ordains that the virgin queen must leave the golden city, where the drones, her own brothers, could have mated with her. She must fly high into the dangerous blue, exposed to the fury of the elements or the attack of a hungry bird. Once in the open air, her scent will inform drones from other hives that she is ready for mating. They will flock toward her, hundreds of them, for each hive contains up to half a thousand males who have only one role to play—the possibility of fertilizing a queen. As the drones converge on the queen, she speeds upward, high above the predatory birds—a glorious skyward journey, the only flight she will ever make until, as an elderly dowager, she will be deposed by a new queen.

The male dies at the moment of fulfillment, but he leaves within the young queen enough seed to fertilize all the eggs she will lay for the rest of her life—which may be as long as five years. When the queen returns to the hive, she is welcomed by the remaining workers. Almost immediately she begins laying, and the orderly cycle of bee life begins again.

The bee family contains many variations from the communal honeybee. Indeed, honeybees did not even exist in America until the early colonists imported them to satisfy a craving for sweets. There are upward of 20,000 separate species of bees and only 5 percent live in colonies. Among the 95 percent (which represent a lower evolutionary stage than the honeybees) are the carpenter bees, living alone in narrow tunnels they hollow out of the pith of sumac or raspberry plants, and the leaf-cutters, so named because of the circular pieces they gouge from rose leaves. The leaf-cutters live alone in cells the shape of a tiny pot made from resin and fastened onto a pine needle. Look for them on any pine tree, and you will probably find more than one.

Many of the solitary bees gather together in colonies to spend the winter. It was probably this nesting instinct which gave rise to permanent communities of social bees, because the bees thrived who had them.

The bumblebees represent an intermediate stage between the solitary and the hive species. The bumbles do not have the intricate organization of the honeybees. Their hives, usually utilizing the abandoned hole of the fieldmouse or chipmunk, are annual affairs. At the beginning of spring the queen lays a few eggs in the shapeless wax cells she has constructed in the burrows—there is no functioning golden city for her as there is for the honeybee queen. She sits alone on her eggs like a brooding hen. When the first workers mature, they immediately buzz out to gather nectar and pollen—you can see the pollen in large, yellow balls on their legs. Some of the bees are so young, they have not yet donned their yellow and black uniform but still wear their drab gray baby color. For a while it is touch and go for the bumblebee village, and even the queen must sometimes take to the field to help feed the developing larvae.

Gradually, however, enough workers are produced to enable the hive to grow to its maximum size, which is usually around a thousand. Perhaps it is this smallness and the intimate contact between the queen and the workers which accounts for the extremely strong attachment felt by the bumblebee for the hive. As part of a routine experiment, I captured a bumble. It was surprisingly easy. I merely put a glass jar over her head while she was engaged with a veronica blossom and, once she was inside, I screwed on the lid from the bottom. When she realized she was caught, she buzzed angrily against the jar sides. But she rather quickly subsided and soon was going about her customary business of gathering nectar from the flower which I had included in the jar. I did not suspect anything when she became very lethargic toward evening. But, to my astonishment, upon returning two days later to observe her, she was dead! When I dumped her out the next day, I found her body already covered with fungus strands, some of which even had the dark dots of their sporangia, indicating they had gone to seed, or to put it properly, to spore. So quickly does nature convert death into new life.

I couldn't believe that this once-vigorous bee had succumbed to the malady of homesickness. So I caught another to observe her more closely. Again she buzzed furiously for a few minutes, then settled down to a growing lethargy. Her abdomen began to curl beneath her. She actually seemed to become deflated—to become much smaller than she had been a half hour earlier when she was free. I prodded her with a twig and got almost no reaction. Then, unscrewing the lid, I placed the jar outside. All she had to do was to fly out. While the open air revived her to some extent, she made no attempt to fly for about twenty minutes. Then she started buzzing against the jar side in a disoriented, hopeless sort of way. She did not fly straight up, so after a while I clamped the lid back on.

She spent the night away from the hive for the first time in her life. As darkness settled on her, she crawled beneath the flower which I had included in the jar and remained in exactly the same position until I found her in the morning. I took her outside and unscrewed the lid again. This time she couldn't even fly. She actually seemed to fear the scented wind. She stumbled to the flower, enveloped herself in the petals—and died.

I repeated this experiment several other times, and with the same results. So unless this was a strange race of bumblebees, it seems likely that their lives exist only in relation to the hive. When taken away from it, they die.

Something similar happens with the onset of autumn. The work-ers sense that their village is breaking up. Although they are large creatures in relation to their honeybee cousins, they are unable to store up enough honey to carry them over the winter. In *Exploring the Insect World,* Teale states that often you will find barely a tablespoon of honey in the entire colony. So as the leaves turn crimson, the work-ers do not return; they just drop dead. The young queens who were born in the colony have already left on their nuptial flights. They will spend the winter beneath some stone or in a hollow log. The old queen ages rapidly, losing all her hair, wanders aimlessly amid the desolation of the empty hive. She has long since stopped laying eggs, and with the first hard frost she too dies. The summertime life of the village is over.

While the bumblebees and honeybees spend most of their lives in their secluded towns, another member of the bee family, the paper wasp, operates out in the open where we can all watch him. Early in the season you will see these wasps (recognizable by the red dot on each side of their abdomens) bounding along house eaves, investi-gating any overhang which may prove a favorable location for their flat, circular combs.

The queen who begins the colony has passed the winter in a sheltered attic or basement cranny. Once she selects a suitable nesting site, she smears a sticky substance on the place where the comb will

be attached, then constructs a narrow paper pedestal—the paper coming from wood she has chewed up. If you are observant, you may see her gouging out tiny mouthfuls from a tree trunk. Then she busies herself laying eggs—although her paltry hundred or less do not compare with the 70,000 or more the honeybee queen lays every year.

At first the workers who emerge from the eggs content themselves with feasting on the pollen and nectar gathered from flowers (as with all bees, they receive protein from the pollen and calories from the nectar). But as the young grubs hatch and demand meat, the adult wasps suddenly turn into ferocious hunters of living prey. Almost no for spiders. These victims, felled by the wasp's rapier sting, are chewed insect is safe from their bloody raids, although their special taste is stage of the butterfly). Henri Fabre, whose patient observations and up and fed to the hungry grubs (which correspond to the caterpillar artful, home-style experiments during the latter part of the nineteenth century made him the authority on wasps, moths, and many other of his "dear insects," was intrigued by the gentleness with which the wasp hunters feed their grubs. "One would never tire," he writes, "of the curious spectacle of these rough soldiers playing the part of tender nurses." They nudge the grubs softly to waken them, then solicitously administer the food they have gathered with such effort.

It is not too difficult to drive the paper wasps from their comb. I have a comb in front of me as I write. It has thirteen neat rows of hexagonal paper cells, with the widest row containing thirteen individual compartments, while those on the extremes have only five. It is light in weight, and the paper rustles as I squeeze it. In some cells I find oblong, whitish eggs pasted to one wall, and on the other side a crystal of nectar. The compartments, incidentally, are open, not covered with wax as would have been the case in the honeybee hive. Many cells are filled with wasp grubs, their large, compound eyes staring at me while their mouths open and their jaws work furiously. These are young killers, hungry for meat.

I soon discard the nest. I don't feel easy with the wasps, for they are too close to the vicious side of nature. The honeybees are more to my liking; their friendly drone is as much the soul of summer as birdsong is the soul of spring.

CHAPTER FIFTEEN

THE DAYS OF
LITTLE THINGS

Ants

"The naturalist," John Burroughs once wrote, "can content himself with a day of little things. If he can read only a word of one syllable in the book of nature, he will make the most of that." I spend many days in my backyard content with the little things. There are the ants, for example, unattractive at first glance, but downright appealing when one gets to know them better.

In many ways ants are more like humans than any other organism on earth. Theirs is not the ephemeral life of a few weeks, as it is with many insects, for the workers live up to four years and the queens thrive for fifteen years—fully as long as most mammals. Nor is theirs a stereotyped existence with predestined duties patterned solely on unreasoning instinct, as with the honeybees, otherwise the closest to man in their civilized mode of living. Ants have the ability to reason out situations that are new to them. They are even closer to us than any of the mammals because they, too, are citizens of teeming cities, are conscientious herders of "cattle," often act as farmers in raising food crops, and function quite effectively in massed, formidable armies.

A city of ants which was situated at the edge of my patio provided me with many interesting days. All would have gone peacefully for them had they not found a cookie my five-year-old-son Jeff discarded on the patio. A few minutes later the cookie was swarming with small, dark red ants. How had they found the cookie so rapidly? I went into my library and began paging through two books I had on ants: Derek Wragge Morley's *The Ant World* and John Crompton's *The Ways of the Ant*. At the same time I started a series of experiments which began harmlessly enough but ended with the ants having quite enough of me and moving away lock, stock, and grubs.

140

The Days of Little Things

My first experiment began the next day when I rubbed my hand over the trail the ants were using to reach another cookie I had placed near their nest. Instantly there was confusion. Large traffic jams piled up on each side of the obliterated track. Most ants just milled around purposelessly. A few, however, began investigating the area around the end of the trail, then set out on their own in the direction the trail used to take. Quickly they reached the other side. More ants followed, and within a few moments the procession was moving freely again.

My experiment had shown two things. The first was that ants depend largely on a scent trail to find their way to a newly discovered food supply—and that by rubbing this trail out, I had destroyed their pathway. My books told me that each ant has an ample supply of formic acid, and when he comes upon food, he will mark his track back to the nest by lightly dabbing this acid onto the earth with his abdomen. Thus the ants who seek to follow his steps have only to scout out the formic acid spots like Indians following a blazed trail. Secondly, I learned to my surprise that most ants are lazy and stupid, and that when the track suddenly disappears, they cannot find their way. On the other hand, a small percentage are what Morley calls "excitement-center ants": bright, energetic ladies (as with the bees all the workers are females) who are the intelligent leaders of their community. It was they who would not accept the fact that their trail was gone and explored ahead until it was re-established.

Another experiment showed more clearly the difference between the average and the excitement-center ants. When I put out a cookie crumb, several of the dullards happened on it first. They nibbled off a piece, then strutted away so pleased with themselves they never thought about returning to the nest with the important information. But when an excitement-center ant discovered the cookie, there was no dallying. She hot-footed it back to the nest where she communicated her enthusiasm to her lethargic sisters, who then began following her formic trail to the cookie.

In still another experiment, I picked up a cookie already loaded with a dozen or more ants and placed it on the opposite side of the nest. Now the ants would not only have lost their original trail, but would have to travel in a completely different direction to return to their nest. Would they be able to get back?

As each ant climbed down from the cookie, she stopped and

waved her antennae, upon which her nose is located, and showed her confusion. Then she zigzagged around trying to pick up the scent trail. Her movements carried her over an increasingly wide area, but still a long way from the actual trail. Nevertheless she was ultimately able to orient herself, and headed off toward the nest.

What had happened? From my readings I learned that each nest has a distinctive odor, and that the ants leave this odor about their environment. Thus foragers can trace their way to the nest by following the general area scent, not a specific trail—the stronger the scent, the closer the nest. In addition, they can recognize many landmarks by sight, for their great, compound eyes serve them almost as well as their highly developed antennae-noses. There is, however, a limit to an ant's ability to return home. When placed beyond the nest scent, she will be hopelessly lost and wander about until she dies.

The nest scent is composed of various elements: first, a species odor passed around as the workers lick a sweet juice produced by their grubs; second, the smells absorbed from the particular material of the nest (dirt, clay, sand, etc.); and third, the odors of the various foods the workers bring home. The entire community is in constant contact with one another, passing these odors around as they exchange a portion of the contents of their communal stomachs (which corresponds to the bee's honey-stomachs). The degree to which food is distributed among members of a community is such that Morley found that when only six of them ate red-stained food, within twenty-four hours the entire colony had stomachs which showed red through their thin outer cover!

While an ant's body may not seem to have enough space for complicated organs, the creature is actually one of the highest forms of life.

The ant's brain is unique among the insects, for the two masses of nerve ganglia usually found in insects have become united into a single large brain. Darwin thought these cerebral ganglia to be of "extraordinary dimensions . . . many times larger than in the less intelligent orders, such as beetles." The greatest biologist was also impressed with the amount of mental activity which takes place within the ant's brain—a brain which occupies an area not so large as a quarter of a small pin's head. "Under this point of view," Darwin wrote,

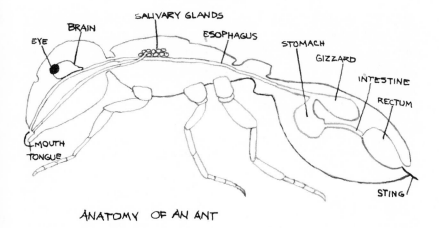

ANATOMY OF AN ANT

"the brain of an ant is one of the most marvelous atoms of matter in the world, perhaps more so than the brain of a man."

Ants, with their remarkable brains and relatively long lives (during which they can absorb and remember many experiences) often act surprisingly like humans. Darwin mentions how they sometimes chase each other in good-natured play. Teale believes each ant has the startling ability to recognize and remember every individual in her nest, the population often running up to 100,000! Like our early explorers, the ants are closely attuned to their environment, particularly to the sun, which they use for orientation as they wander over great distances in search of food. And they have an almost human sense of time, since they adjust their directions according to how far the sun has traveled across the sky since dawn.

Yet despite her complex body and acute perception, the ant is a remarkably sturdy animal. Cut off her head, and the remainder of the body will live for twenty days. Leave her head with a pair of legs, and the little head will run off, alive and active. She can live without food of any sort for well over a month and can remain under water for upwards of a week!

But back to my experiments. Ant societies are so successful that, like those of man, they have few real enemies except themselves. Ant wars are fairly common. They are usually fought over territory. Normally ants are not hostile toward those of a different nation when

143

they meet during foraging. Even when an alien approaches the home nest, there is little animosity. To verify this I placed a light red ant from a nearby nest close to the dark red camp. The light red stood quite still, her antennae flickering as she probed her new surroundings. When a dark red bumped into her, they tapped each other gingerly, then the light red hurried off, even though there was no apparent sign of hostility between them.

Real wars usually begin in hot weather when the ants' tempers are ready to flare. Two foragers from different nations meet and fight over food, which each believes to lie within his own territory. Soon they are joined by others and a general conflict begins. I tried to instigate such a conflict by placing a cookie an equal distance away from both the light red and dark red nests, but the dark reds found it first and when the light red scouts discovered that their neighbors had already taken possession of the cookie, they left it alone.

Undaunted, I gathered together two cookie-loads of ants, one from each nest, and placed them together in a closed plastic container. I waited expectantly, but there was no battle. Evidently neither group felt the other was trying to infringe upon its territory. Instead, the two groups merely tapped antennae, then went about the more serious business of trying to find a way to escape. When I returned the following morning, the light and dark red ants had gathered together in a corner with no hint of hostility between them. Presumably an interchange of odors during the night had accustomed them to each other.

Actually they were beginning to merge into a new race, and that is not too uncommon among ants, for more than one race sometimes live together. Several excitement-center leaders from each group began working in unison to construct an underground nest in the sand I had placed at the bottom of the container. They worked quite hard the first day, and managed to dig out a tunnel several inches long even though some of the less intelligent ants greatly hampered them by picking up the granules which they dumped right back in the tunnel mouth!

Yet life is a strange and unpredictable thing. The tough little ants, who can live with their bodies severed, or under water, who will fight like tigers against any intruder no matter what his size—these ants, without a queen, will quietly expire, even though there is plenty of food available. And so, after three days, my ants curled up

144

and died—and all that remained of the formerly active little insects were twenty crumpled bodies.

The queen is the key to the ant civilization. Ant communities are more provident than those of their near relatives, the honeybees, for most nests contain more than one queen. The ubiquitous Pharaoh's ants have up to 2,000 queens, which explains why they are so difficult to eradicate once they are established in a home. Instead of expelling the old queen when a new one is born, the ants not only let her remain, but actually seek additional queens to insure an ample supply of workers. Since each ant queen can lay up to 1,000 eggs a day and may live for as long as fifteen years (as compared with only five years for a queen bee), one can see how the ants have a far greater potential for expansion than the bees.

The geographical expansion of the ant cities comes several times a year when thousands of winged princes and princesses issue from the nest. At the house where I grew up it was quite a sight to see the countless—literally countless—flying ants come rising from the base of the lilac bush in which the nest was located. But the ants, being weak fliers, are carried along willy-nilly with the wind. And birds by the score are waiting for them in greedy anticipation. It is a real feast and many birds fall to the ground, unable to fly, because their stomachs are so weighed down with the ants they have consumed. For the ants who escape, mating occurs in the air. The queen often requires as many as six male contacts to provide her with sperm enough for her many years of laying.

When the mating is completed, the male falls to the ground, where he lives a pathetic, purposeless existence until he dies several weeks later. For the queen, on the other hand, life has just begun. She must find a suitable location in which to start her nest. There are no scouts to help her, as with the honeybee swarm. Unless she is adopted by a colony in need of more queens, she will dig herself a small chamber beneath a rock. Once the chamber is completed, she closes up the opening and for the next ten months lives a life of privation inside her self-imposed tomb.

This is the crucial period. She lays her eggs and has to await the emergence of the workers. During this time her only food will come from the muscles that supported the wings which she ripped off shortly after her marriage flight. She will eat some of her eggs if the going gets really rough, but, of course, she must save enough to start the colony. When the eggs hatch, they are not ants as we know them, but small white grubs, completely helpless. The queen must share her food with them—such as it is. At last the grubs spin fawn-colored cocoons, and within them undergo a metamorphosis as complete as that which alters a caterpillar into a bright-winged butterfly. When they wiggle out of the cocoons, they are very pale in color, extremely stunted from lack of food, and their exterior plate of armor, which will eventually harden, is soft and flabby. However, they are able to push aside the pebbles covering the nest to begin foraging for much-needed food. Yet often it is too late, for the weakened queen may die at the very moment of success. Of all the thousands of young ants who soar bravely out of the original nest only one, on the average, will survive to begin a new nest. Such is the toll nature takes to insure that only the hardiest will survive.

During the summer I frequently watched "my" ants trail in and out of the nest beside the patio. Through my magnifying glass I watched them tapping antennae in friendship when they met; I watched them exchanging food from their communal stomachs; I watched them laboring home with particles of food larger than themselves; and I watched them struggle through the grass-forest, over the scorching sand, past the dangerous, folded leaves where the sticky nets of the spiders waited for them. I got to know their haunts, their favorite resting places (for ants enjoy a leisurely rest, just as we do). And at times I felt as though I could see the world through their eyes.

One of their favorite feeding grounds was in a stand of tall gloriosa daisies. But the flowers meant nothing to them. The attraction was the immense numbers of aphids that clung to the stems, sipping the juices that flowed upward. Aphids are greedy little bugs: fat, globular, tiny as pinheads when born, but increasing rapidly in size until they are as large as many ants. During the summer they are all females, reproducing more females without the necessity of male fertilization. Their reproductive capacity is fantastic. In almost any colony you can find scores of young issuing from the abdomen of their feeding virgin mothers. The aphids have only two purposes in life—to reproduce and to feed. They move only when their source of supply is depleted. They are so intent upon feeding that they consume far more liquid than they can digest. The surplus is constantly ejected in the form of droplets known as honey dew which often coat the windshields of cars parked under elm and willow trees.

Long ago the ants found that honey dew was delicious, and it became their staple food. To control the ejection of the liquid, the ant strokes the aphid gently along the bottom of its abdomen. This is a delicate art—Darwin tried it using the finest hairs in his possession—and failed. The ant, however, knows how to coax the aphid to issue the liquid slowly enough so that she can collect it in her communal stomach. After imbibing from four or five aphids, the ant will head back to the nest, her abdomen much distended.

Ants are conscientious caretakers of their aphids, which have been compared to our herds of dairy cattle. Watch them for a while —the aphid-tenders are common in almost any garden—and you will see them drive off the aphids' numerous enemies, such as the lady bugs who can consume up to thirty aphids an hour. But the ants' protection does not end here. When summer storms arise, many species of ants bring the aphids right into their nests to protect them from the weather. And in the winter, aphid eggs are stored in the security of the ant nest until they hatch in the spring.

But in spite of all my snooping and spying, I still had an intense curiosity. I wanted to know what the interior of the nest looked like. So one day late in August I removed the small, flat rock under which the entrance path led. Beneath the rock I found a large chamber almost an inch wide and one-quarter inch deep. There were about fifty ants there—some active, others just resting. The night had been cool so they had brought dozens of their young (both the white larvae and the brown cocoons) to this upper chamber to enjoy the heat transmitted by the sun-exposed rock. As soon as I removed the rock, they began frantically carrying the larvae and cocoons into a broad passage which led downward.

Following the tunnel with my trusty trowel, I went down a few inches, veering to the right with the tunnel. There I came upon another large chamber. This one was completely stuffed with larvae and cocoons. It was about the same size as the first, but because it had been built amid a layer of stones, it had a completely different character. Every speck of dirt had been excavated from the area, leaving the chamber walled with lovely stonework: red, white, and speckled black, as artfully fashioned as the interior of a cathedral.

Ten minutes later, after the harassed ants had cleared the chamber, I removed the rocks and continued digging. Now I found two equally large tunnels running down at almost a 90 degree angle. They were both smooth and spacious—evidently major thoroughfares. I took the one to the left and three inches later uncovered another storage area. The ants were already removing the young, for the news of my catastrophic arrival had obviously spread throughout the entire nest. I found some queens here, easily distinguished by their slightly larger and lighter bodies and long, fat abdomens. The royal ladies leisurely ambled among their scurrying workers, disdaining to aid them in their frantic work.

For more than an hour I delved deeper and deeper within the nest. It had seemed such a simple affair when I began, but now I had a hole nearly a foot deep, and just as wide. I was able to uncover seven galleries, yet still the radiating tunnels led downward. I found the general direction turned so that I was beginning to undermine the patio. As evening came, I abandoned my work in defeat.

But the episode was not yet over. The ants had had enough of my meddling. Sometime that night the excitement-center leaders had decided that the colony should seek its fortune in a less risky environment. With this decision reached, the bosses began trooping out of the nest at dawn, carrying eggs, larvae, cocoons, and any workers who disputed their leadership. The procession was long—several yards— and continued through most of the day. As with a colony of humans, there was a certain amount of resistance among the conservative element, and many of the ants who had been bodily carried to the new abode, hit the trail back to the old nest—for them there was no place like home, mutilated though it might be.

Nevertheless, the excitement-center leaders were not to be thwarted. By the next day, the old nest was completely deserted. I had my hole and a pile of dirt, but my ant colony had moved to an inaccessible location amid some rocks surrounded by silver king artemisia. Reluctantly I shoveled the earth back in the hole. I had enjoyed watching the little citizens of another civilization, and now the patio seemed empty without them.

But a backyard is filled with so many day by day little happenings that rejection by a colony of ants cannot dampen one's spirits for long.

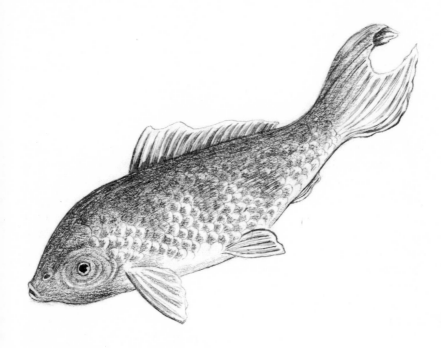

CHAPTER SIXTEEN

ASCENT TO THE THUMB

The Evolution of Vertebrates

*T*he animal world has two great divisions constantly at war with one another. The insects represent the highest development of one of the divergent lines; the other is man. Insects follow only their instincts. Flies, mosquitoes, and beetles have been able to compete very effectively with man. Other insects—the bees and ants—again using only instinct, have been able to create societies far more stable and better organized than man's bickering, often warring world. Using intelligence instead of instinct, man is usually on the defensive, barely able to control the hordes of insects which eat his crops, his clothing, his houses, and respond to his insecticides by developing new, resistant forms.

Insects and man—let's examine their differences. The insects have three distinct body divisions—head, thorax, and abdomen—whereas man has only a head and torso. Insects have six appendages, while man has only four. Insects breathe through tiny tubes in the thorax and abdomen, man through his large lung sacs. Insects have wings; man, of course, has none. Internally, the insects have blood, but it is not red, for it does not contain hemoglobin or carry oxygen. Insects possess no capillaries or veins to transport the blood back to the heart. The blood simply circulates freely through the cells. The insect's nervous system consists of a double nerve cord running down his underside, rather than a single cord along the upper side as with man. Humans have a strong backbone upon which the bony skeleton is anchored. The insects have no such interior framework; their support comes instead from an exterior covering upon which the muscles are attached.

A spinal column composed of vertebrae segments is the distinguishing feature of the division of animals to which man belongs;

indeed, that division is referred to as the vertebrates. A backyard offers a surprisingly suitable location to study the evolution of the vertebrates. We begin with our old friend the earthworm, for the current theory is that the vertebrates descended from an earthworm ancestor, and the following reasons are given: the blood-flow is the same in the two types of animals, both have a single nerve cord, and the vertebrates have curiously segmented excretory organs distinctly similar to the segmentation so obvious in the earthworm. In addition, the earliest known vertebrates are tongue worms, small soft-bodied animals living in shallow water.

A step above the tongue worms are the goldfish—swimming about so merrily in my pond. In the goldfish I find an animal close to me in evolution: its eyes are like mine, the teeth are similar to mine, the brain is in a bony cranium like mine, and in the fins I see harbingers of my own limbs.

And the goldfish respond to me. When I first placed them in the pond, they hid at the bottom whenever they saw me. Gradually, however, they learned to come when I sprinkled food on the water. And a few even grew so used to me that they did not flee when I stroked their sides as they lay relaxing beside a lily leaf. Certainly this was far different from the reactions toward me by the earthworms or snails.

Although goldfish are similar to humans in many respects, there are just as many differences. They have ears, but hear only faintly— for acute hearing did not evolve until land creatures were able to escape the muffled, semisilence of the water. Their ears serve primarily to keep them in balance; their hearing, such as it is, comes from a row of sense organs in the lateral line which runs along each side of their bodies. Obviously, the goldfish has a method of obtaining oxygen that is quite different from ours. We can see him filtering water through his gills, which are filamented structures where capillaries bring the blood in close enough contact with the inflowing water so that an exchange of carbon dioxide and oxygen can take place. While it may appear that the fish is swallowing immense quantities of water, actually all the liquid passes through the gills and the only water to enter the stomach comes when he gulps down the vast quantities of mosquito larvae he finds so delicious.

Many fish, including the goldfish, have a large, thin-walled sac

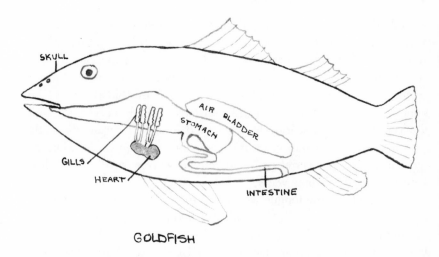

GOLDFISH

near the middle of their bodies called an air bladder, which enables the fish to achieve better depth control. During geological times some fish began using these bladders to breathe, and it was from such ancestors that human lungs eventually evolved. While man's lungs clearly demonstrate his fish heritage, even more surprising is the fact that we still have rudimentary gills, readily apparent on the developing human embryo.

Slowly certain lung-fish evolved into a new species known as amphibians, which belonged half to the land and half to the sea. The pond frog is a good example. While he may appear to be very much at home squatting on a mossy stone, he is really quite dependent on water to stay alive. His skin must always be moist, for even when he is out of water part of the oxygen he needs is absorbed through his skin, and in the winter during hibernation under water, his entire air supply comes through his skin. When the young hatch out of the eggs, they are not frogs, but tadpoles—those dark, flat-headed creatures that breathe by means of gills (not with lungs, as adult frogs do) and resemble fish in everything except grace of movement.

Yet the evolution of the frog was quite an accomplishment. In order to walk on land, he had to have well-developed limbs rather than frail fins. He needed well-functioning lungs. He had to have ears to hear with, eyes protected by lids from the dusty air, and vocal cords to call to his mate. The first music ever heard might have been the croak of a frog.

Then came the day of the reptiles. While they developed from certain froglike ancestors, they were far better adapted for land life. Perhaps the greatest "invention" of the reptiles—one that made it possible for vertebrates to live on land—was the development of the hard-shelled egg. The amphibians were always forced to return to the water, for exposure of their soft, jellylike eggs to the elements would have been catastrophic. But the reptiles could wander far from the sea, and when the time for egg laying came, the female could deposit her tough-coated eggs in the sand or among rocks.

These eggs, whether they belonged to the ancient dinosaurs or to the ancestor of the turtle who lives in my pond, were truly amazing devices of nature. In a sense the reptile egg carried the ocean with it, since it furnished its own liquid. The yolk sac furnished an ample larder of food, and the respiratory membrane took care of filtering the precious air to the embryo. Safe in this miniature world of its own, the reptile baby could develop in security and plenty until it was ready to crack through the shell.

As the reptiles began to move far out over the land, they began to develop powerful legs for locomotion. In a very real sense, then, we can thank the turtle and his ancestors for our walking facility. Of course the reptiles did not consciously strive for powerful legs. It was simply a matter of "natural selection," to use Darwin's term: those

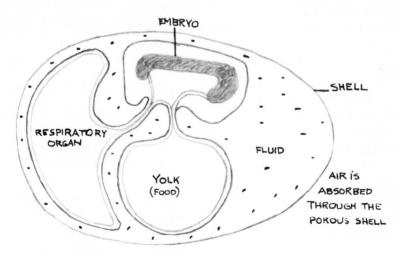

REPTILE or BIRD EGG

with better legs were better equipped to procure food. With the land open and inviting, the more agile reptiles moved farther and farther inland, stimulating the need for stronger and stronger legs.

It was the same with another reptile "invention." Because they lived so far from water, they needed a thick skin to retain the precious moisture. And so the development of scales began. Snakes are still covered with a scaly coating, and a turtle's shell is nothing more than a fusion of many separate scales.

But natural selection, or survival of the fittest, was not the only factor guiding the evolutionary process of reptiles. As Darwin was quick to point out, many animals possess structures which not only are valueless in the battle to survive, but on the contrary, often are serious hindrances to continued life of the species. The alteration of the quick-moving reptiles into ponderous dinosaurs, so huge and bizarre that they were unfit to meet the changes in their environment, illustrates the factor that Darwin called sexual selection. Apparently, oddities of scale decoration were considered beauty marks by the dinosaurs, assuring them of a mate—so that the greater the oddity, the more certain it was of being passed on to future generations. In this manner the once-agile lizards were gradually transformed into clumsy monsters.

Now they are all gone—all those bellowing, grotesque creatures. Yet their line lives on in the meek, retiring turtle who suns himself on a flat rock in the midst of my pond. Like the former titans of the plant world, the club mosses and the ferns, he too fears the step of a five-year-old child; he too shrinks from the world his ancestors once dominated.

From the reptiles, the vertebrate line evolved in two directions. One division changed the heavy scales into the light, fluffy structures we know as feathers. This line became the birds. The other division remained earthbound. Scales altered into fur, and somehow the blood of the mouselike creatures who were the first mammals became warm. This was a most startling development, since never before (except for the birds who were emerging during this same period) had any species been able to maintain a constant body temperature. Previously, the animal had always been utterly dependent upon the weather.

But the mouse did not experience these difficulties—at least not to nearly so great a degree. Warm blood and the alteration of noninsulating scales into fur enabled him to maintain his activity no matter how cold it became. This meant that he could resist the sudden changes in temperature that caught the reptiles off guard. And so the warm-blooded little mouse survived while the thundering dinosaurs passed into oblivion.

As the ages rolled on, the advance of the vertebrates continued. At about the same time that the first flowers were putting in their appearance, the scurrying mice began differentiating into new, larger forms. Soon other rodents began to appear: squirrels, beaver, and the closely related rabbits. Then came fleet-footed horses and the ruminants: cattle, deer, and sheep. Dogs evolved, as well as the cat family, including the fearsome sabertooth tiger.

But the most important line, as far as man is concerned, was that of the monkeys and apes. These animals lived mainly arboreal lives, and their forelimbs altered from the paw of other vertebrates to fingers with an opposable thumb which enabled them to secure a firm grasp on the limbs of trees. This opposable thumb was one of the great breakthroughs which led directly to the development of man. It is intriguing to wonder what would happen to our laboriously erected civilization should the thumb and fingers suddenly revert to a paw. It would be impossible for us to run machinery, to plant grain, to pick apples, or even turn the pages of a book. It may be that the human hand is the most wonderful organ created by evolution—with the thumb its most important part.

CHAPTER SEVENTEEN

THE WORLD'S MOST MARVELOUS FLYING MACHINES

The Structure and Psychology of Birds

*T*o all who hear the robin's constant twitter or watch a host of English sparrows fluttering around a feeder, there seems to be little mystery about birds. After all, they are so common; we have grown used to them; they are simply part of our environment, like the elms and the drifting clouds. But actually a bird is quite an unusual creature. It is difficult to believe that the bird evolved from the clumsy, heavy-footed reptile—but that is actually what happened. Scientists have found fossil remains of prehistoric birds from which they have reconstructed a weird half-reptile half-bird that gives some idea of the bird's ancestor. This creature was about the size of a modern pigeon. His wings were long and awkward; his mouth was lined with vicious teeth; he had a long, bony tail, and his head and neck had scales instead of feathers. His wings were still used partially as forelimbs, since there were well-developed claws at the ends of them. This archaic bird could probably scamper up trees and glide from the branches, but it had little power of actual flight. When creatures better able to fly evolved, this original stock, unable to compete with them, died out.

As evolution continued, the reptilian scales altered into feathers. The change was of great value, for it provided the birds with an excellent covering that weighed next to nothing. And the lack of weight enabled them to achieve better flight.

It was necessary for birds to keep their weight to a minimum since they had to rely on flight to survive. Therefore, they had to give up teeth, normally essential in defense. These were replaced with a lighter gizzard where the food was ground up by means of small grains of sand and pebbles which they had swallowed.

Other alterations were necessary, too. The female could not be weighed down with a large supply of eggs—as was the case with fish and reptiles. Instead, her eggs matured at spaced intervals so that she could lay them one at a time—and there were far fewer, usually less than six, rather than hundreds as with the fish.

But there were advantages to the active, alert life which flight brought about. The brains of birds expanded and their sight grew exceedingly keen. Most birds can see at least eight times better than man. Even small song birds have eyes that outweigh their brains; and the largest eye on any land vertebrate belongs not to the elephant but to the far smaller ostrich.

Of all the adaptations of birds for flight the most surprising is their bone structure. Whereas our bones are filled with marrow, the bones of birds are hollow—and therefore much lighter. Although this in itself is strange, odder still is the fact that these hollow bones serve as tubes conducting air—thus functioning as part of a bird's breathing mechanism. A bird does not breathe the way we do—by sucking air into large, space-wasting lung-sacs. When a bird breathes, the air continues right into its bones, eventually reaching the farthest wing tip. To relate this to man, it is as if each breath he took sent air as far as his big toe.

To be capable of flight, birds were forced to develop other unusual characteristics. To flutter their wings the muscles must move with a quickness which is almost convulsive. And to maintain the needed energy, a bird must keep a very high body temperature—like a racing engine. A bird's temperature is usually over 105 degrees, sometimes as high as 115 degrees. (Perhaps this will impress you when you remember that bath water at 115 degrees will burn you.) A huge heart pumps this heated blood around the bird's body with startling rapidity—beating three times faster than a human heart when the bird is in flight. And to provide fuel for this torrid body, the average bird must consume food up to twice its weight each day. For a human to "eat like a bird" it would be necessary for him to gorge himself with 200 hamburgers for breakfast, 200 more for lunch, and another 200 for supper—buns and all!

Probably the most appealing characteristic of birds is their song. "I heard a robin in the distance," Thoreau wrote as spring came to Walden Pond, "the first I had heard for many a thousand years, methought, whose note I shall not forget for many a thousand more."

A "silent spring"—to use Rachel Carson's chilling words—would be a tragedy even to those who have little appreciation for bird song.

The songs of birds have long been associated with love calls—and certainly their plaintive melodies seem akin to our own ballads. Yet even in this most familiar aspect of bird life, there is another interesting element. Usually only the males sing well, and the songs are used not only to attract the female, but also to announce to all other males that the territory belongs to the singer. Robert Ardrey, in *The Territorial Imperative,* indicates that most birds sing only within the borders of their own particular domain. Thus it may be accurate to state that the call of the male is primarily an aggressive assertion: a challenge rather than a sentimental love song. Darwin reports that the drive to sing is so overwhelming that it is not unusual to see a bellowing male bird drop dead from a ruptured blood vessel!

Another odd fact about the singing is that usually the small bird's call is the finest. It almost seems that the fine singing compensates for lack of size. It is strange too that birds sing without vocal cords. Instead, they have a special set of reedlike muscles deep in the chest, which vibrate as they force air over them. By varying the tension in these muscles (which no other animal possesses) notes of different pitches are produced.

Bird coloration relates to evolution. No doubt, to begin with, in order to escape detection, the coloring of birds was drab. Yet birds prefer bright colors even as humans do. When occasionally male birds differed from the dull norm, the brighter feathers proved attractive to the less numerous females, and they were able to mate more easily. Since the female had to remain exposed in the nest during the incubation of her eggs, it was the male who survived the handicap of color. Thus, according to Darwin, sexual selection produced birds with bright plumage.

One of the most interesting aspects of bird behavior concerns migration. Edwin Way Teale, driving through Florida in early spring, found the state swarming with birds ready to begin the trek back to their northern breeding grounds. "We saw robins flying, robins perching, robins running across lawns, robins swarming over fire-blackened open spaces among the palmettos. For miles on end we would see robins all about us." And there were bluebirds, and clouds of swallows, and trees alive with blackbirds.

Most migrating birds have the uncanny ability to find their way back to the particular nook they left nearly six months earlier. They time their migration to keep pace with the food supply: hummingbirds wait for the unfolding of flowers; robins for the emergence of worms from the earth with the end of winter; and warblers anticipate the birth of caterpillars. Except when over water, birds do not fly long distances. Warblers, for example, average around 23 miles a day. Most migrants are chubby with fat. The long journey will not be easy, for in addition to the constant hazard of insufficient food, there are storms to battle, hawks to evade, sickness to overcome. The weak will fall by the wayside. And even after the northern breeding grounds are reached, there are new homes to build, more food to gather, families to rear, and competition with the stubborn English sparrows who had all winter in which they could consolidate their hold on the choice nesting and feeding sites.

There is nothing particularly mysterious about the migrations in the autumn: food has become scarce, and instinct, based upon an ancient survival pattern, guides the birds sunward out of the now bleak land. But how do they know it is time to return, for it is always warm in Florida? Helmut Adler in *Bird Behavior* describes an experiment with some juncos which answers this question. By the use of artificial lights the birds were made to believe the day was lengthening—as it would in the spring. It was found that this change in light induced a rapid growth in the birds' reproductive systems, preparing them for the mating that would normally occur at this season. When the juncos were released, they immediately migrated north toward their mating grounds.

Birds seem to find their way by using the sun. This was proved by a German scientist who confined a group of starlings in a circular cage from which only the sky was visible. The birds were trained to take food from one of twelve identical containers. When the sun shone, the starlings could always find the right container. But when it was overcast, they made mistakes. To further verify the starlings' reliance on the sun for directions, an artificial sun was made by shining a light bulb through cheesecloth. The birds then used this new "sun" to guide themselves, and established a completely new set of directions. Night-flyers, such as warblers, wrens, and humming-birds, probably use bright stars in place of the sun. Some migrating birds, particularly those over the ocean, may guide themselves by the magnetic field which circles the earth—but this has not yet been proved.

There is also this question: if the birds have been living success-fully in the southlands, why do they undertake the arduous and perilous journey to the cold north? Why not just remain in the south and breed there? The answer must be that the crowded conditions in the south would not permit the tremendous increase in population that takes place when each pair of mated birds releases five to ten times their number to live off a limited supply of food. In this sense migrations are an instinctive operation designed to prevent a situation which has not yet arisen. Nature likes to plan for the future.

CHAPTER EIGHTEEN

RETURN OF THE VAGABONDS

Bird Migration

*O*ften I have looked out of my window and pitied the robin hopping through a thin blanket of snow, forgetting that he is not a warm-weather fanatic like many of the birds who follow. Snow and sleet are not disturbing, for he does not come north seeking warm weather—that is purely incidental. It is the worms he is after, and the worms come to the surface when the average temperature is 35 degrees. For this reason the hardy robins always move northward into a climate that is just above freezing.

Early colonists named our robin after a European bird, but one with a far redder breast. They came to know our robins well, for these friendly birds were attracted to the small, worm-rich clearings the settlers were making in the forested wilderness that had been inhospitable before to both white men and birds. As the farmers and their wives labored in the fields, they began to cherish the melodic evening serenade of the songsters which reminded them of the distant homes they would never see again. Perhaps in unconscious imitation of our pioneer ancestors we, too, value the robin above all other birds.

The male robin will arrive first each spring in order to establish uncontested rule over a sufficiently large area to support his prospective family. Each male will try to rule an area of about four house lots, with some neutral ground in between. Let any interloper approach, and you will see him driven away with an angry cry and a quick flurry of wings. Oddly enough, each male recognizes the realms of his competitors, and when he intrudes in these territories his fighting spirit dwindles and he permits himself to be ushered homeward— perhaps by the very bird he drove out of his own kingdom a few moments earlier! "Possession of a territory," writes Robert Ardrey in his superlative book *The Territorial Imperative*, "offers some mysterious advantage usually sufficient to guarantee victory for the defender."

When the females arrive, courting begins, and the songs take on an added zest. A robin's song is unmistakable: up and down he trills, playing with two basic note levels as if he were talking to himself. Once the female (who can be recognized by her slightly paler coloration) chooses her mate, she starts nest-building. While many species are content with rearing one brood a year, the robins will often launch three: one in May, one in June, and if the weather remains tolerable and food plentiful, a third in September. The male refuses to help his mate construct the nest, but his aid isn't necessary, for she works very fast. Robert Ardrey reports how a gardener hung his coat up at 9:15 one morning, then returned at noon to find a nearly completed nest in the pocket.

Yet for all their effort in raising the young (the male is very active in obtaining food) the male and female robins seem to have little real affection for each other. They pair only for the breeding season, and when it is over they go their own way.

Once the robin arrives, he is here for the season. But there are vagabond birds who come to my yard, linger for a short time, then are off—to return the next year, or two years later, or, perhaps, never.

Around the first of April a flock of cedar waxwings usually appears. They are handsome, tailored birds, confident, supercilious aristocrats, chatting together in high nasal tones while they dine on the red berries of my snowball bushes. Their dress is impeccable: soft brown plumage with conspicuous head-crests, breasts of a tasteful yellowish hue, and wings tipped with bright red the color of old-fashioned sealing wax, which gave them their name.

They eat, they twitter, they buzz into the air after an early fly or two—then thirty minutes later they are gone—to return again a year later on the very same day, almost to the hour.

Far different is another bird that visits me in mid-April. I see him contentedly tramping through the oozing mud at the base of the honeysuckle. He is a strange-looking fellow who teeters like a drunk as he walks, with a tuft of white feathers in place of an actual tail. His body is rather large but is topped with an unusually small head. This is a sandpiper—but not the kind you see strutting along the ocean beaches. This is a solitary sandpiper, part of a subspecies who prefer the inland marshes. He is usually alone, a hermit bird, who utters a plaintive little cry as he flies off. For this reason he is also called the solitary tattler.

Various types of sparrows arrive early too. At first glance they look almost identical to the common English sparrows—who actually are finches, not sparrows at all. But I notice that their habits are strikingly different even before I am aware of the color differentiation. Easiest to tell are the white-crowned sparrows. During April I grow accustomed to watching them eat dandelion seeds—something I have never seen the English sparrows do. They attack the pods that hold the seeds like a puppy shaking an old sock, while their heads, which are lined with the three white bands that give them their name, bob rapidly. Once I went over to examine one of the dandelions, and almost all the seeds were gone. Here certainly was an effective weed killer.

The white crowns are on their way to their Canadian breeding grounds. After a week at most they will depart by way of Wisconsin, where the lumberjacks have long been calling them streakheads.

Another dandelion-eating member of the sparrow family is commonly known as "chippie" for his pleasant chirping song. The chipping sparrow has a solid reddish crown which also helps identify him. Often a pair will remain all summer, but I usually see them only during a week or two of spring.

Most pleasant of all are the song sparrows. For many years they have made my Aprils and Mays (and often the entire summer) brighter with their bubbling song usually done in triplets. They are dull-colored birds with no vivid markings—only a spotted breast and a long, constantly bobbing tail which distinguishes them from their much more numerous English sparrow cousins. Yet they do not particularly care for seeds (because their beaks are soft) and you can pick them out as they flit around in search of insects.

If the song sparrow's appearance is undistinguished, his melody is not. To Thoreau, the song sparrow's melody seemed to reveal the ardent hopes of the young year. Teale loved the song for its robust quality which contained none of the sad dreaminess of other songsters. No two males ever sing exactly the same way, yet John Burroughs listened to one warble from morning till night and found it repeated the same lyrical phrases over and over. I myself have spent many pleasant hours in my garden enjoying the sunshine and the continuous serenade of a song sparrow. He never seemed to tire. I felt his joy and it made me feel good too.

Not all birds come from great distances. Many juncos (even though they have a black hood and white breast, are still part of the multitudinous sparrow family) have remained here all winter. About the first of April their numbers are greatly increased by the addition of tribal members from a few miles south. The air is filled with them, the small white wedges that appear on their tails when they fly brightening the yard as if they were pieces of silver. But by mid-April all the juncos are completely gone. They will eventually migrate as far north as the Canadian tundra where they will build their nests on the semifrozen earth amid the desolate, wind-buffeted landscape, preferring the brisk climate to the muggy, overheated southern weather.

As the juncos leave, their place is taken by the warblers—a fair exchange. The warblers bring the tropics to my home. Their sweet songs seem to speak of their winter hideaways in Panamanian jungles, Costa Rican savannas, or the lush coffee-lands of Colombia—places I too remember with pleasure. The warblers are true transcontinental vagabonds—not stay-at-homes like the robins, sparrows, and so many of our birds.

"Nothing in the world is more alive than a warbler in the spring," writes Teale. Their songs are melodic outbursts filling the air. Most impressive are the yellow warblers, often called wild canaries. They come in large flocks, almost taking over an area. A few are quite tame. More than one has walked right under me as I sat in a lawn chair. At other times they have landed on some floating seaweed in my pond only three feet away where they splashed and frolicked, pausing only now and then to dart upward after a butterfly or to perch on a flower stem and pick off some aphids.

About the same week that the warblers arrive, another tribe begins showing up—the finches. Undoubtedly the most spectacular is the goldfinch, often confused with the yellow warbler, and often called, too, the wild canary. Teale saw more than a hundred of these bright yellow birds, with the black caps that distinguish them from the warblers, pausing on their migration flight to rest in a cypress beside

Florida's historic Suwanee River. The sky was somber with threatening clouds, but the twittering, active birds made the day seem gay: "like a smile breaking on a lowering face."

The goldfinches usually arrive just in time to take part in what John Burroughs, one of our most lyrical nineteenth century naturalists, aptly calls a dandelion festival, which occurs around the first week of May in my neighborhood. Just as the pesky dandelions begin to dot the lawns and sweep over the vacant lots, the goldfinches descend on them, several dozen at a time. This is probably the most spectacular bird display of the year. They will perch right on the dandelion stem and peck away at the seeds. After the main course is over, they flit among the bushes, consuming hundreds of unwary insects. Later on, when the long-stemmed gloriosa daisies open, they return in small flocks to light on the stems and pick off the endless colonies of aphids that are sucking the juices from the helpless flowers.

Nesting usually does not begin until the thistles open, for the finches like to line their nests with soft thistledown. In one of Audobon's most pleasing pictures, he draws the finches clinging to a swaying thistle while they pluck at the strawberry-colored plumes of the flower heads. Indeed, it is so common to see the birds around these plants that they are often called thistlebirds.

Charles Darwin uses the male goldfinch's elaborate courting display to illustrate the degree to which the female, almost always duller than the male (the female goldfinch is brown rather than yellow), helped to develop the brilliant plumage in males through her selection of the more colorful one for her mate. "When he courts the female," Darwin writes, "he sways his body from side to side, and quickly turns his slightly expanded wings first to one side, then to the other, with a golden flashing effect."

But while the coloration of the goldfinch is eye-catching, the songs are just as endearing. Many times during springtime, often far into the night, I have heard a finch or two trilling in the distance—a soothing sound almost canarylike. It rings through the quiet air like vesper chimes struck rapidly but lightly. It is a melodious summation of spring, still untouched by the jaded overtones of late summer.

As spring moves on, other birds begin to frequent my little domain. A pair of catbirds have been nesting in the honeysuckle bushes for the past three seasons. Burroughs relates a story of how a friend so tamed a catbird that it would fly into her dining room to receive a lump of butter she would hold out on a fork. Although I have not been able to develop such a comradeship with my catbirds, they do perch quite close, chattering and mewing (from which they get their name) as they thrash through the bushes.

Of course, the bluejays are always around, the rasping nasal call hardly in accord with their trim azure and white coloring. Now and then a pair of cardinals hop across my yard, and later I hear their shrill, tuneful whistle from a distant tree—reminding me of long-ago days when I slept on a back porch looking up into the many-storied branches of a silver maple where another pair of cardinals sang throughout the summer.

There are swifts, too, that zip across my field of vision continuously. Almost never alighting—they are completely creatures of the air. They circle high above like hurled boomerangs, around and around, especially toward evening, catching mosquitoes and other insects in their large mouths, which are always open as they fly. The atmosphere vibrates to their constant chittering from mid-May, when they arrive, until they depart as the last insect dies in autumn.

The swifts are truly amazing birds. Some of the Old World swifts have been clocked at nearly 200 miles an hour, and I myself have stood among Inca ruins and been buzzed by swifts that bolted so close that I could hear the low hissing caused by the velocity of the downward plunge. Unlike almost any other bird, the swift beats its wings alternately like a swimmer, and perhaps this brings about the truly remarkable speed. The original nesting sites of swifts were in hollow trees, but when man came along, they found his chimneys better, so they took up summer residence there. John Burroughs, in his tireless pursuit of bird knowledge, crawled into the base of a tall chimney through a narrow opening left by the removal of an old steam boiler. He saw approximately ten thousand swifts propped up along the interior of the fifty-foot structure by means of their short, spiny tails. Amid the constant shower of droppings, he was able to watch their actions:

The sound of wings and voices filled the hollow shaft. On looking up, I saw the sides of the chimney for about half its length paved with the restless birds; they sat so close together that their bodies

169

touched. Moreover, a large number of them were constantly on the wing, showing against the sky light as if they were leaving the chimney. But they did not leave it. They rose up a few feet and then resumed their positions upon the sides, and it was this movement that caused the humming sound. All the while the droppings of the birds came down like a summer shower.

A detailed description of the other birds visiting my garden could go on and on. There were scores of grackles, of course, those big, long-tailed blackbirds with an oily-bluish sheen and voices that are imitations of their unlovely name. An oriole appeared for several days, three years in a row, showing in its orange and black plumage the colors of Lord Baltimore, for whom the early colonists named it. Woodpeckers of all sorts—red-headed, downy, and flickers—tried their luck at my willow tree. Red-winged blackbirds, who must have strayed from their prairie homes, occasionally sat on my fence. Several times I heard the distant song of a meadowlark, although certainly a city area of four million people is an unlikely place for such a creature. A towhee scratched around my feeder like a chicken for fifteen minutes one spring. Groups of starlings—those squeaking, unpopular birds imported from Europe in 1892—swarmed into my yard at frequent intervals. And many wrens have perched on top of my wren house—and even though they are not supposed to be fussy about their abodes (John Kieran reports they nest anywhere: in mailboxes, clothespin bags, or the pocket of an old coat) I have never been able to attract a family.

But the most exotic bird to call on me is undoubtedly the ruby-throated hummingbird. No other bird is able to hover like the hummer—and he can even fly backward when the necessity arises. He prefers to take his food on the wing, and as he hovers beside a flower he uses his unusual tubular tongue like a straw to siphon up the sweet nectar. The hummer, strictly an American bird, is the smallest non-insect flyer in the world; his weight is rarely as much as a penny, and a half dollar will completely cover his nest. The nest is an ethereal thing, matching the bird itself, for it is made of soft mosses and spider webs, and is concealed on twigs by lichens.

The hummers, exotic as they may seem, are actually somewhat common. There has not been a year that one or more has not fre-

quented my garden. I will be sitting quietly, and suddenly the little
bird is hovering nearby on a snapdragon, his wings beating so fast I
cannot see them—I can hear only a low hum. There is a magical quality
about him, he is so silent and stationary, as if he were a painting, not
a living creature. His tail is open, as he steadies himself in the air, and
there is a strange, greenish luminescence to his back. Then before I
have time to blink, he is sipping from another snapdragon many
feet distant.

One of the most astonishing things about the hummers is their
fearlessness. Although their three-inch length makes them little larger
than some insects, they will often attack other birds many times their
size; and they show no fear of humans. Once when I found a female
(whom I recognized by her dull color and white rather than ruby
throat), I was able to bring my hand to within six inches of her. She
stared at me, unafraid, and I believe I could have touched her had
I dared.

Too often we take birds for granted. We have grown accustomed
to seeing them bouncing over our lawns or soaring through the sky.
Yet the ways of man do not always harmonize with the routine that
nature has ordained. As Rachel Carson reminds us, it is possible that

we may unwittingly—through pollution of the water, the air, and the soil—bring about the extinction of our winged friends.

Even without modern pollution, man has already extinguished more than one species. John Burroughs tells of seeing vast armies of passenger pigeons migrating across the country each spring. The sky would become fuzzy blue with their feathery bodies, and the air would reverberate to the sound of their soft, childlike calls. The gigantic flocks covered the trees, the bushes, and even the homes and barns. Audubon, watching a migration of pigeons, estimated there were over a billion in the single flight.

Man, convinced that such bounty could never end, caught the trusting birds with nets or batted them down with clubs. It was a game, a spring and autumn festival. Entire towns turned out in the fields to slaughter the nearly tame pigeons.

Then one day the pigeons' nesting instinct was destroyed. With the flocks disorganized and decimated, they somehow lost the will to reproduce. The last great flight was in April, 1875. The next year Burroughs came upon a lone passenger pigeon, which he shot, little dreaming that he should never again see one alive. It happened with startling quickness. One year there were billions, and the next year just a few lonely stragglers. Zoos began gathering the remaining birds, but race suicide had gone beyond recall, and they would not reproduce even within the security offered them. The last passenger pigeon died in 1914.

Now they are gone forever. Man with all his modern scientific wonders can never re-create a single one of the pigeons that once swarmed over the country. It is a regrettable story, but one with a moral. The danger still exists that other species of birds may become as extinct as the passenger pigeon. Perhaps we should consider the words of Burroughs:

> What man now in his old age who witnessed in youth that spring or fall festival and migration of the passenger pigeons would not hail it as one of the gladdest hours of his life if he could be permitted to witness it once more?

CHAPTER NINETEEN

AUTUMN

*A*s with any empire, the one which exists in my backyard has a rise, a climax, and a fall. Spring was the time of growth, of reaching for the clouds. Summer brought a fulfillment, a blaze of color, a gay flamboyancy, as if the era would never end. But autumn comes at last, and the decline begins.

There is an uneasiness about autumn that few can deny. My pond goldfish grow lethargic; the snails sink to the muddy pond bottom to begin their hibernation; the water lilies no longer send flowers up through the mass of bespotted leaves. The honeybees have stopped visiting the withered summer flowers, and the acrid, though brilliant chrysanthemums have little appeal to their sweet tooth. Wasps wander about purposelessly, for their nests are breaking up. The fireflies are gone, and the crickets chirp slowly in the cold, seemingly aware that their lives will be extinguished with the first frost.

The entire character of the flower garden has changed, too. The familiar flowers of deep summer are on the wane, as they require the long daylight hours to produce their finest blossoms. On the other hand, new plants thrive on the short days. Most varieties of salvia, asters, dahlias, and mums will not flower until the daylight is less than 13 hours, and this, not the onset of cold weather, is the crucial factor causing them to bloom.

During the ancient days of Europe, while the Celtic inhabitants were still pastoral, the Druid priests kept careful track of the setting position of the sun so that the herders would know the accurate, astronomical time of the season, and would not be fooled by a prolonged period of warm weather. The Druids knew the grass would begin to wither with the end of October, so they lighted great bonfires to warn the scattered tribes that the time had come to gather together the

wide-roaming herds and lead them to winter shelter in their barns—
or possibly inside the homes themselves. Gradually this autumn fire
festival became one of the chief ceremonies of the Celts. Every village
and farmhouse had its bonfire on October 31st, the traditional day
when the herds were brought in.

But along with the herds came less wanted guests: the ghosts of
the dead, who wished to come into warm homes for the winter. Thus
the 31st was a night when old crones, or witches, would speed through
the air and all the forces of evil and death would hover maliciously
in the darkness. The bonfires were kept burning, not only to brighten
the darkness but, perhaps, as sacrificial pyres to placate the spirits of
death—for the original bonfire actually meant "bone-fire." When Christianity came to these lands, the fearful night was named All Hallows
Eve, or Halloween, but superstition still prevailed, and even today,
for all purposes, autumn ends with the howling of witches on
October 31st.

Yet with all the mystery and uneasiness about autumn, there are
still those wonderful days of Indian summer, the most glorious sub-
season of the year. Then the warmth of deep summer returns for a
brief holiday; the air is mellow and fragrant with the smoke of burning
fires; and the trees are painted in the brilliant war-paint of departed
Iroquois, Chippewa, or Sioux.

This is the halcyon time: the time when the mythical halcyon
bird took advantage of the unusual warmth to raise a quick brood.
"The days take on a mellower light," Walt Whitman wrote, "and the
apple at last hangs really finish'd and indolent-ripe on the tree. Then
for the teeming, quietest, happiest days of all! The brooding and
blissful halcyon days!"

Nowhere else in the world is there an Indian summer: it is
strictly an American mixture of our sugar maples, our dry yet hazy
weather, and our Indian heritage. "This halcyon period of our autumn
will always in some way be associated with the Indian," John Burroughs noted. "It is red and yellow and dusky like him. The smoke of
his camp-fire seems again in the air. The memory of him pervades
the woods." Yet, since this is so, I wonder why we persist in our story
that it is Jack Frost who paints the leaves? Why not an old Indian
medicine man riding through the countryside on the wings of Mudje-
keewis, the strong West Wind? With a brush of beaver fur, using dyes

from wild berries, making his designs from pictures on warriors' chests, he works day and night, a cunning, wizened fellow, his face lined with three hundred summers, and in his memory the long space of time before the white man came. Then Indian summer would have more meaning.

But science has robbed us of our mythology. Actually it is not the frost that paints the leaves. In a manner of speaking, the leaves are golden during the entire growing season—summer as well as fall. The color is made by two chemicals: carotene, an orange-yellow pigment found abundantly in carrots, and xanthophyll, the sunny substance that brightens the wings of canaries as well as the yolks of eggs. The yellows are always in close association with chlorophyll, and for this reason are believed to aid in photosynthesis. The green of the chlorophyll generally obscures the yellows—but if you destroy the chlorophyll, by placing a stone or piece of wood over some grass, you will find the yellows there even in the summer.

However, in autumn the chlorophyll dies most completely, revealing the yellow pigments. One essential factor in the destruction of chlorophyll is the shortening of the day, which induces the formation of an abscission layer between the leaf stem and the twig which supports it. This layer cuts off the flow of nutrients into the leaf, and thereby prevents the addition of new chlorophyll to replace that which is used up in the normal process of food manufacture.

Another factor that produces the pleasing autumn gold is dryness. I observed this myself by watching the progress of two identical maples. One of my neighbors watered his tree conscientiously; the other did not water his maple at all. On October 8th the watered maple was still completely green, while the dry one was beginning to turn yellow. By the fifteenth, the watered one was still as green as ever, but the dry one (it had not rained in two weeks as is usual for October here) was half yellow. After the first frost on the twenty-third, the watered one began showing fringes of brown, but the dry one continued to sport a pleasant, golden canopy. By November 8th both trees began to lose their leaves: the watered one its leaves of drab brown, the dry one its bright foliage of tan. Both trees had been exposed to the same weather, but the colors had been radically different.

The formation of the flaming reds is quite another matter. The

reds are produced by compounds known as anthrocyanins which are carried in the cell sap and bear no association with the chlorophyll. Indeed, they are not generally present within the leaves until a special set of circumstances comes about. First, there must be the erection of the abscission layer which impedes the removal of sugars manufactured in the leaf. Second, there must be a sudden drop in the evening temperature accompanied by the third factor, a series of dry and sunny days which together promote the breakdown of the sugars into the red anthrocyanins. That. these brilliant dyes are actually mere waste products of sugar destruction need not detract from our appreciation of the beauty they produce.

Because intense sunshine is necessary for the reds to reach their fullest splendor, maples sometimes are crimson in places exposed to the sun—one side perhaps, or possibly just at the ends of branches— and golden in others. This accounts for the somber European autumns where the mild and cloudy weather does not promote the formation of the anthrocyanins. Incidentally, it may not be out of place to point out that the anthrocyanins are also responsible for the reds, blues, lavenders, and purples of many flower petals.

From the blaze of October, I watch autumn fade into less flamboyant November. Often the days are still Indian-summer warm, and the air is fragrant with smoldering bonfires. Leaves cascade around like dry waterfalls and children who play in them shout with as much glee as if they were great snowbanks. Meanwhile high above, the trees begin to stand bare and brown, swaying with a lithesome grace I had forgotten.

The shadows lengthen until they stretch gauntly across my backyard, reaching even to the bed where snapdragons once stood in perpetual sunlight. Now, if I wish to sit in the yard, I have to search out a spot in the sun, knowing that even here the broomlike motions of the tree-shadows will follow.

Then the temperature drops. A sheet of ice forms a death mask over the pond and the first flakes of snow spin furtively by. It is time, I realize, to make one last survey of my garden.

BIBLIOGRAPHY

American Museum of Natural History, *Natural History* Magazine, various issues.

Ardrey, Robert, *African Genesis.* New York, Dell Publishing Co., 1961.

———— *The Territorial Imperative.* New York, Atheneum Publishers, 1961.

Asimov, Isaac, *A Short History of Biology.* N. Y., Natural History Press, 1964.

Audubon, J. J., *Audubon's Birds of America.* New York, The Macmillan Company, 1950.

Bastin, Harold, *Freaks and Marvels of Insect Life.* New York, A. A. Wyn, 1954.

Berrill, N. J., *The Living Tide.* New York, Fawcett World Library, 1956.

Blunt, Wilfrid, *Tulipomania.* Harmondsworth, Middlesex, England, Penguin Books, 1950.

Bradshaw, John, *Guide to Better Gardening: Annuals.* Toronto and New York, Leland Publishing Co., n.d.

———— *Guide to Better Gardening: Biennials.* Toronto and New York, Leland Publishing Co., n.d.

———— *Guide to Better Gardening: Perennials.* Toronto and New York, Leland Publishing Co., n.d.

Burns, Eugene, *The Sex Life of Wild Animals.* Toronto, Rinehart and Co., 1953.

Burroughs, John, *John Burroughs' America.* Garden City, N. Y., Doubleday and Company, 1951.

———— *Pepacton.* Boston, Houghton Mifflin, 1881.

———— *Under the Maples.* Boston, Houghton Mifflin, 1921.

———— *Winter Sunshine.* Boston, Houghton Mifflin, 1875.

Carson, Rachel, *The Sea Around Us.* New York, Oxford University Press, 1951.

———— *Silent Spring.* Boston, Houghton Mifflin, 1962.

Crompton, John, *Ways of the Ant.* Boston, Houghton Mifflin, 1954.

Cruickshank, Allan, *The Pocket Guide to Birds.* New York, Dodd, Mead, 1953.

Darling, Lois, and Darling, Louis, *The Science of Life.* New York, Bantam Books, 1961.

Darwin, Charles, *The Descent of Man.* New York, Modern Library, n.d.

My Backyard

Darwin, Charles, *The Origin of Species.* New York, Modern Library, n.d.

de Kruif, Paul, *Microbe Hunters.* New York, Harcourt, Brace & World, 1932.

Fabre, Henri, *The World of J. Henri Fabre.* New York, Premier Books, 1956.

Farb, Peter, *The Forest.* Life Magazine Nature Library, New York, Time, Inc., 1961.

——— *The Insects. Life* Magazine Nature Library. New York, Time, Inc., 1962.

Fisher, Robert Moore, *How to Know and Predict the Weather.* New York, Harper and Bros., 1951.

Fox, H. Munro, *The Personality of Animals.* Harmondsworth, Middlesex, England, Penguin Books, 1947.

Frazer, Sir James George, *The Golden Bough.* New York, The Macmillan Company, 1922.

Free, Montague, *Gardening.* Garden City, N. Y., Doubleday and Company, 1954.

Frost, S. W., *Insect Life and Insect Natural History.* New York, Dover Publications, 1959.

Fuller, Harry J., *The Plant World.* New York, Henry Holt and Company, 1951.

Gooch, Bernard, *The Strange World of Nature.* London, Lutterworth Press, 1950.

Gottscho, Samuel, *A Pocket Guide to Wildflowers.* New York, Dodd, Mead, 1951.

Hamilton, Edith, *Mythology.* New York, New American Library, n.d.

Harlow, William M., *Trees of the Eastern and Central U. S. and Canada.* New York, Dover Publications, 1942.

Hausman, Leon Augustus, *The Bird Book.* Greenwich, Conn., Fawcett, 1955.

Hylander, Clarence J., *The Macmillan Wild Flower Book.* New York, The Macmillan Company, 1954.

Kieran, John, *An Introduction to Birds.* Garden City, N. Y., Garden City Publishing Co., 1946.

——— *An Introduction to Nature.* Garden City, N. Y., Hanover House, 1955.

——— *An Introduction to Trees.* Garden City, N. Y., Garden City Publishing Co., 1954.

Kimble, George, and Bush, Raymond, *The Weather.* New York, Penguin Books, 1946.

Lane, Frank, *Animal Wonder World.* Greenwich, Conn., Fawcett, 1957.

Life Magazine, *The Wonders of Life on Earth. Life* Magazine Nature Library. New York, Time, Inc., 1961.

——— *The World We Live In. Life* Magazine Nature Library. New York, Time, Inc., 1955.

Locy, William, *A Story of Biology.* Garden City, N. Y., Garden City Publishing Co., 1934.

MacDonald, J. D., and others, *Bird Behavior.* New York, Sterling Publishing Co., 1962.

Maeterlinck, Maurice, *The Life of the Bee.* New York, Dodd, Mead, 1912.

Bibliography

Mellersh, H. E. L., *The Story of Life*. London, Arrow Books, 1957.

Morley, Derek Wragge, *The Ant World*. Harmondsworth, Middlesex, England, Penguin Books, 1953.

Murchie, Guy, *Song of the Sky*. Boston, Houghton Mifflin, 1954.

Peattie, Donald Culross, *Flowering Earth*. New York, Viking Press, 1939.

————, and Peattie, Noel, *A Cup of Sky*. Boston, Houghton Mifflin, 1945.

Peterson, Roger Tory, and Fisher, James, *Wild America*. Boston, Houghton Mifflin, 1955.

Platt, Rutherford, *A Pocket Guide to the Trees*. New York, Dodd, Mead, 1952.

———— *Walt Disney's Worlds of Nature*. New York, Simon & Schuster, 1957.

Quinn, Vernon, *Stories and Legends of Garden Flowers*. New York, Frederick A. Stokes, Co., 1939.

Reed, Chester A., *Bird Guide*. Garden City, N. Y., Doubleday and Company, 1946.

Rogers, Julia, *The Tree Book*. New York, Doubleday, Page & Co., 1905.

Sanderson, Ivan T., *How to Know the American Mammals*. New York, New American Library, 1951.

Seymour, E. L. D., ed, *The Wise Garden Encyclopaedia*. New York, William H. Wise & Co., 1959.

Shapley, Harlow, and others, *A Treasury of Science*. New York, Harper & Bros., 1943.

Simpson, George Gaylord, *The Meaning of Evolution*. New Haven, Conn., Yale University Press, rev. ed. 1967.

Smith, Ellen Thorne, *Chicagoland Birds*. Chicago, Chicago Natural History Museum, 1958.

Storer, John H., *The Web of Life*. New York, New American Library, 1953.

Stuart, Frank, *City of the Bees*. New York, McGraw-Hill, Inc., 1947

Teale, Edwin Way, *Autumn Across America*. New York, Dodd, Mead, 1956.

———— *Exploring the Insect World*. New York, Grosset & Dunlap, 1944.

———— *Journey into Summer*. New York, Dodd, Mead, 1960.

———— *North with the Spring*. New York, Dodd, Mead, 1960.

Thoreau, Henry David, *Walden*. New York, New American Library, 1949.

Winchester, A. M., *Biology and Its Relation to Mankind*. Princeton, N. J., D. Van Nostrand Co., Inc., 1964.

Wright, Richardson, *The Story of Gardening*. New York, Dodd, Mead, 1934.

Zim, Herbert S., *Birds*. Golden Nature Guide series. New York, Simon & Schuster, 1949.

———— *Flowers*. Golden Nature Guide series. New York, Simon & Schuster, 1950.

———— *Insects*. Golden Nature Guide series. New York, Simon & Schuster, 1951.

———— *Mammals*. Golden Nature Guide series. New York, Simon & Schuster, 1955.

———— *Trees*. Golden Nature Guide series. New York, Simon & Schuster, 1952.

INDEX